Osprey Modelling • 33

Modelling the T-34/76

Jorge Alvear, Mig Jimenez, Mike Kirchoff & Adam Wilder

Consultant editor Robert Oehler • *Series editors* Marcus Cowper and Nikolai Bogdanovic

First published in Great Britain in 2006 by Osprey Publishing
Midland House, West Way, Botley, Oxford OX2 0PH, UK
443 Park Avenue South, New York, NY 10016, USA
Email: info@ospreypublishing.com

ISBN-10: 1-84176-929-0
ISBN-13: 978-1-84176-929-5

Page layout by Servis Filmsetting Ltd, Manchester, UK
Typeset in Monotype Gill Sans and ITC Stone Serif
Index by Alison Worthington
Originated by United Graphics Pte Ltd, Singapore
Printed and bound in China by Bookbuilders

06 07 08 09 10   10 9 8 7 6 5 4 3 2 1

A CIP catalogue record for this book is available from the British Library.

FOR A CATALOGUE OF ALL BOOKS PUBLISHED BY OSPREY MILITARY
AND AVIATION PLEASE CONTACT:

NORTH AMERICA
Osprey Direct, C/O Random House Distribution Center, 400 Hahn Road, Westminster, MD 21157, USA
E-mail: info@ospreydirect.com

ALL OTHER REGIONS
Osprey Direct UK, P.O. Box 140 Wellingborough, Northants, NN8 2FA, UK
E-mail: info@ospreydirect.co.uk

www.ospreypublishing.com

Photographic credits

The photographs that appear in this work were taken by the following contributors:

AW	Adam Wilder
DP	Dave Parker
JA	Jorge Alvear
MA	Mosin Alexandr
MJ	Mig Jimenez
MK	Mike Kirchoff

Acknowledgements

Jorge Alvear:
I wish to acknowledge the time and effort put forth by Paul Gibson and Mark Rethoret in helping me get the details correct for the Factory 112 T-34/76 featured in this book. Their help was invaluable. Thanks also go to Mark Neville, a friend who I consider one of the most talented model painters today; I am fortunate he was willing to paint the model for me. Thanks also to Chris 'Toadman' Hughes for his T-34 picture CD, which is excellent; Jon Tamkin and Michael Rinaldi at Mission Models; and especially Michael Szapowalow at Air Connection. My contribution to this book is dedicated to my wife Rebecca, who has made my life as complete and fulfilled as I could have ever hoped.

Mike Kirchoff:
I must acknowledge Nicola Cortese, whose trust and faith opened this door for me. For that, I will be both eternally grateful for having been given the opportunity and, more importantly, for his friendship. This project also would not have happened without the guidance of Mark Rethoret. He exhibited tremendous patience when tasked with answering each and every mundane question I posed, while also providing me with priceless reference material regarding the T-34. Thanks for keeping me pointed in the right direction. Lastly, I'd like to thank Mosin Alexandr, whose awesome photographs of 'Sniper' inspired me to tackle this daunting task. A true gentleman, without his talents behind the lens I would never have had the clarity to attempt this project. I dedicate my contribution to this book to my best friend, my muse, my wife, Linda. For 28 years her patience and understanding, along with a keen eye and unrelenting demand for perfection, has continued to support and challenge me to be the best I can be. My indebtedness to her for this, and many other things, is without measure.

Adam Wilder:
I would like to thank the following people: my father Jeff Wilder and friend Daniele Guglielmi for proof-reading and helping me to edit my chapter; Daniele Guglielmi for his advice, photos and information on my T-34/76; Miguel Jimenez for his advice and help with the tarps; and Ed Bernardo for the photos. I would also like to thank my mother Gail, my brother Ryan, and my uncle Steve Loignon for all their encouragement and support.

Mig Jimenez:
I would like to thank Adam Wilder for his help on the Aber grille for my T-34 project. I dedicate my work to Nicola Cortese, who opened up the possibility for us all to work together on this book.

Contents

Introduction

This is a 1/35-scale Factory 112 T-34/76 from late 1942, built by Jorge Alvear and painted by Mark Neville. (DP)

The T-34 was the most influential tank design of World War II, with its sloping armour, heavy hitting firepower and rapid mobility. It first saw combat in the summer of 1941, and its qualities soon set it apart from other medium tanks of the period. However, its battlefield superiority did not last long, and it was soon matched by German designs such as the Panther. Several models, designated by years, were produced between 1940 and 1943, featuring changes such as upgunning (Model 1941) and redesigning the turret (Model 1943). More T-34s were produced by the Allies than any other tank. The T-34/76 was produced until mid-1944, when it was replaced with the better-armed T-34/85.

The modelling community is well served with numerous full kits and a plethora of aftermarket items to cater for the interest in the T-34/76, and it remains one of the most popular World War II Allied modelling topics with new kits being released. The aim of this book, which features the work of some of the world's leading modellers, is to guide the reader through the principles of assembly and finishing the T-34/76 in 1/35 scale, as well as detailing more advanced construction and painting techniques.

T-34/76, Factory 112, 1942

Subject:	T-34/76 from Factory 112, Krasnoye Sarmovo, Gorki, autumn 1942
Modellers:	Jorge Alvear (construction); Mark Neville (painting)
Skill level:	Advanced
Base kit:	Dragon 6205 T-34/76 Model 1941 with glacis from Dragon 6203 T-34/85 UTZ Model 1944
Scale:	1/35
Additional detailing sets used:	Aber AB35045 T-34/85 Detail for Dragon kit
	Aber AB35A45 T34 Fenders 1942-45
	Aber AB35A97 T-34/76 Rear Large Fuel Boxes
	Aber AB35G11 T-34/76 Model 1940 Transmission Cover
	Aber AB35L34 T-34/76 1941–1943 76.2mm F-34 Aluminium Barrel
	Artisan Mori MRP10 T-34/76 Early Type Drive Sprockets
	Chesapeake Model Design CMD42 T-34/76 Model 1941 Cast Turret
	Modelkasten MASK34 T34 Model 1941 Tracks
	Moskit MOS3506 T34 Exhaust Pipes

Construction
The hull and running gear

Quite a few changes were required to accurately represent a Factory 112 T-34/76 produced in 1942. Dragon has a Model 1941 and a T-34/85 kit, but no actual 1942 version; so it was necessary to kitbash these two together. This was simpler than it appears, as I only needed to add the glacis from the T-34/85 kit to the hull of the Model 1941. However, the weld seam between the glacis and hull was actually interlocking, rather than flat. Unlike the STZ T-34/76, however, the rear hull did not also have an interlocking join. To reproduce this unique weld seam, the entire area was puttied with Tamiya putty, then sanded completely smooth after the putty had dried. I used my Dremel tool with a small disc on it to carve out a trench along where the interlocking weld seam would run. Milliput was rolled into a long thin tube and placed into the trench, made flush using a hobby knife, and then patterned with a small syringe that has the end filed into a half-moon shape. This technique was introduced to me by Lee Lloyd.

The specific T-34/76 that inspired me had appliqué armour on the hull, to offset the more powerful cannons on the German tanks introduced in 1942. This was made using plasticard of the appropriate thickness, cut out and filed to fit over the glacis details. A weld seam was then made around the entire appliqué armour, again using Milliput. The armoured nose of the hull was made with Evergreen 0.25in. tube (6.3mm), split in half and glued to the front. A thin strip of 5-thou plasticard was placed along the middle part of this tube, and Milliput sealed the open ends of the tube. The nose was then textured and weld seams added along the upper and lower edges. The sides where the idler wheel sits also had an interlocking join; this was represented by carving out a trench with the Dremel, a small bit of plasticard was placed there, and the seams cleaned up. The hull machine gun is a 22g spinal needle, and Royal Model screws replaced the plastic model versions around the periphery of the mount.

The T-34/85 glacis has been fitted to the T-34/76 hull; note also the Tamiya putty used to fill in the gap on the sides. Spare track mount locator holes were puttied over. (JA)

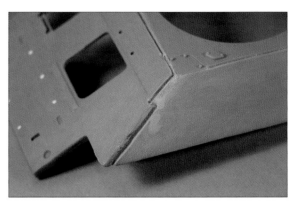

The new trench for the interlocking weld seam, seen in Factory 112 T-34/76s. It was formed using a small disc in a cordless Dremel drill. The weld seam was made from Milliput and a filed-down syringe. (JA)

This picture shows the items I use for surface texture. I apply the Mr. Surfacer 1000 from Gunze Sangyo with a nylon brush, since it is stiffer and holds up better as I stipple the surface. (JA)

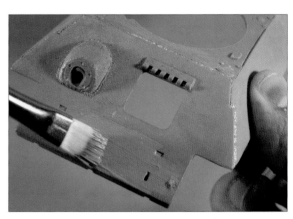

Here I am applying the Mr. Surfacer, brushed on in a thin coat. However, Mr Surfacer dries 'tight' to the surface so it is not strictly necessary to give it a very thin coat. The aim is to give a little depth to the texture. (JA)

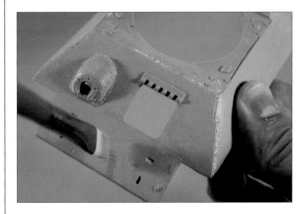

Stippling the surface using a nylon brush, poking it into the Mr. Surfacer repeatedly in a perpendicular fashion. Notice the interlocking weld seam on the hull. (JA)

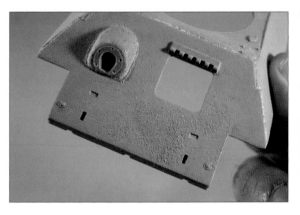

The glacis surface after the stippling. It has a very rough finish, but sanding it gently will create the desired texture. Note the incomplete hull machine-gun mount weld seam; there should be a gap in the front. (JA)

The texture of the glacis after judicious sanding. Some areas are a bit rougher, some a bit smoother. The surface of the hull machine-gun mount is meant to be very rough as this was a cast item. Note the new 'nose' of the T-34 at the bottom, made from a plasticard tube. (JA)

This picture shows the appliqué armour made from plasticard. After this was placed on the glacis, a weld seam was added along the edges. (JA)

Along the sides of the upper hull are thin strips of plasticard in an L-shape, which represent splash guards, another hallmark of Factory 112. Were it not for the appliqué armour on the front hull, there would have been splash guards along the upper edge of the glacis as well. The Aber fenders were used on the sides, but the front fenders were left off due to the prevalence of this feature on T-34s in photographs. The side fenders were welded to the hull not as a long weld but interrupted; this was replicated using Milliput. The toolboxes are from the Aber set, as is the two-man saw and its rack.

Along the rear half of the hull, the transmission cover was redone, using the Model 1940 cover. While this model represents a Model 1942 T-34/76, there are multiple pictures in my references showing the presence of a Model 1940 cover on Factory 112 T-34/76s, evident by the presence of latches rather than two hinges on the rearmost part. The bolt detail in the area of the vents is poor and so these were shaved off and replaced with new bolts made with the Historex hex punch and die. The vents are Aber photoetch; the instructions would have you place bolted covers at the edges of the vents, but pictures show they were actually placed within bulges that were part of the hull. I represented this by filing a small divot to accept the vent edge, and then placing a very small amount of putty over it.

The rear hull required several changes to represent a Factory 112 vehicle. Foremost among them is a rear plate that overlaps the lower edge, rather than butting into it. For this some plastic surgery was necessary, with the lower hull edge sanded back a bit and a whole new rear plate made out of plasticard. The centre area for the access hatch was opened by drilling out multiple holes within the area I wanted open, and then joining them and sanding out the circle to the desired diameter. Bolts were again made using the Historex, and the torch cuts were represented by pushing the Micro Chisel into the plastic softly, along the edge. The large fuel tanks are from Aber, and the exhausts from Moskit. One important last detail of the Factory 112 rear hull is the hinge of the rear plate. Rather than sitting flush, the hinge is actually 'off' the hull to a certain extent, and the lower part has three knuckles rather than one. A set of hinges from Tank Maker were used, with some alteration. Lastly, a towing pintle was scratchbuilt and added to the lower rear hull; these are often found in Factory 112 T-34s.

The only alterations to the Dragon running gear were Artisan Mori drive sprockets, which are very attractive, and Modelkasten tracks. The latter are very cleanly cast and improve the overall look considerably. They are tedious to assemble, but the results are worth it.

The turret

The turret used was the CMD T-34/76 Model 1941 Cast Turret (CMD 42). It is very nicely cast, with minimal clean up, but there are multiple changes required to match it to a Factory 112 cast turret. First, the hatch at the back was not present on the cast turret from Factory 112, so this detail was sanded off and the gaps filled in. Also, the CMD turret tapers down along the upper rear part, so this had to be levelled off; there was no taper on the Factory 112. Tamiya putty was used liberally, and this allowed me to sand a nice edge and eliminate the taper. The Factory 112 turret also had the late-style ventilator and the PTK-5 turret periscope. These two excellent items were generously provided by Mark Rethoret, and they added a lot to my model. The hatch itself had to be completely scratchbuilt as the Factory 112 hatches had a unique 'hourglass'-shaped boss. I made the hatch and the hourglass part, glued them together, and then blended the edge with Mr. Surfacer 500 and some judicious sanding.

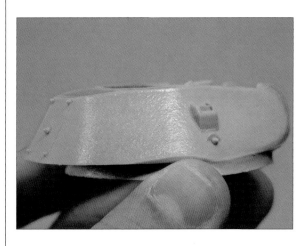

The Chesapeake Model Design Cast Model 1942 turret. A lovely piece of work – but it is an STZ turret and will need to be reworked to portray a Factory 112 cast turret. (JA)

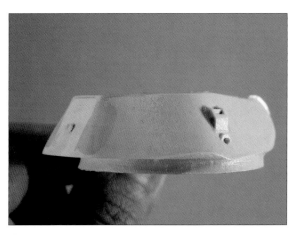

The reworked rear part of the turret, with the bolts removed, the plate gap filled in, and the upper edge squared off. The pistol port was retained. The side casting seam will have to be removed and redone. (JA)

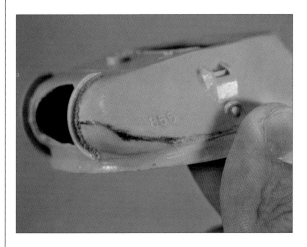

The cast numbers I added to the turret side and the marked area of the future side casting seam. The numbers were shaved from kit sprue. The weld seam where the front turret meets the projection that protects the recuperator housing needs to be removed. (JA)

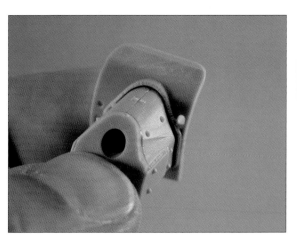

The recuperator placed into the kit mantlet. As you can see, the weld seam from the kit is off from the recuperator edge and the upper recuperator edge needs a weld seam as well. (JA)

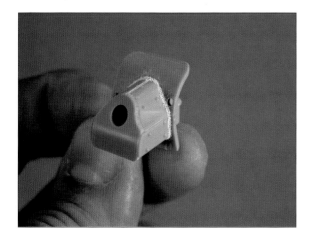

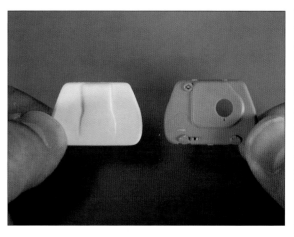

This picture shows the recuperator with new weld seams in the midline above and below, and along the edge attached to the mantlet. The torch cut marks were made by gently pushing the Micro Chisel into the edge. (JA)

The new turret hatch made of plasticard on the left, with the hourglass shaped centre, and the Model 1941 kit hatch on the right. Further details were added to the new hatch prior to placement. (JA)

Factory 112 cast turrets, as seen in the pictures of the Polish 1st Armoured Division, showed four-digit casting numbers on the sides. To portray this I made numbers by shaving off some sprue, glued them in place, and then textured them lightly with Mr. Surfacer 1000. The casting seams along the sides of the turret had to be rescribed, so that they ran straight under the pistol port with a steeper upward curve into the mantlet. Also, the lifting eyes had to be relocated to within the weld seam on the upper turret, so they were on the turret roof plate itself. Grab handles on the turret and hull were fabricated using the Grabhandler, a tool that makes it very easy to make reproducible lengths. The Factory 112 grab handles were unique in that they were mounted using return bends rather than separate brackets. The barrel is from Aber and it fits perfectly within the Dragon recuperator. It even has rifling inside the bore! The recuperator itself received all-new weld seams, as the ones on the kit leave a gap in that area. Also, weld seams were added along the midline of the upper and lower recuperator housing. Torch marks at the front edge were made using the Micro Chisel once again. The coaxial machine gun was drilled out for a more realistic appearance.

Texturing techniques

When considering how to achieve the look of rolled versus cast steel, I was heavily influenced by Makoto Takaishi, who, in one of his articles, stressed the importance of attaining accurate texture. He wrote that it is important for the surface not to be consistent, but rather for it to have some smooth areas and some rougher ones.

For reproducing the texture, I use a nylon brush and Mr. Surfacer 1000. I use a nylon brush because it is a little stiffer than a conventional one and allows me to stipple the surface more effectively. Mr. Surfacer 1000 is a form of thin liquid putty and is perfect for this task. After I have stippled the surface and it has dried, I sand it with 280-grit sandpaper, leaving some areas smooth and some areas a touch rougher. When reproducing a cast surface, such as the turret of this model or the hull machine-gun mount, I paint on the Mr. Surfacer, stipple it, let it dry, and then put on another coat in the same manner. This way when I sand it down lightly, some areas are quite uneven in a manner that well represents cast steel. A final advantage of this technique is that if you are not happy with the results, you can sand it off and redo it, unlike when using liquid cement for adding texture.

Working with photoetch and soldering

To me photoetch is very useful in detailing a model, in that it better represents scale thickness and also allows for damage to be easily reproduced. There are many companies that produce photoetch, but for me Aber is the manufacturer of choice. Several different Aber sets were used in this kit, mainly because the kit was bashed together from two offerings, thus requiring pieces from different sets.

Photoetch is best attached to plastic using cyanoacrylate (CA) glue; you can join two pieces of photoetch together with CA too, and it will stay together quite well. However, for optimum strength and also to fill gaps on segments joined together at right angles, such as a fender curve or a storage box, soldering really is the method of choice. When I first tried soldering I struggled mightily, more a reflection of the soldering tools used rather than the technique itself. Currently I use a cordless rechargeable soldering iron from Wahl Clipper and Tix Solder and Tix Flux, all purchased from Micro Mark. I also use the superfine Micro Tip in the soldering iron as it allows the best control.

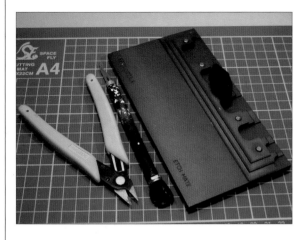

Here are the tools I use for photoetch work: a Xuron photoetch shear; a hobby blade; a cutting mat; and the Mission Models Etch Mate, for bending pieces of photoetch. (JA)

How to make hinges from photoetch using the Etch Mate. This technique allows for quick and easy hinge construction, since the pieces are held down tightly. Fine-tip tweezers are used to bend the arms of the hinge around the wire. (JA)

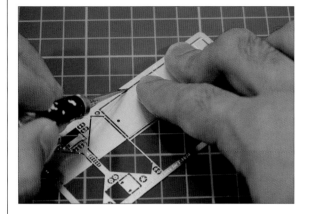

The first step of assembling an item from photoetch: cutting it off the sprue with the hobby blade. It is advisable to cut each item just off the edge of the specific part, thus avoiding damage to the part itself. (JA)

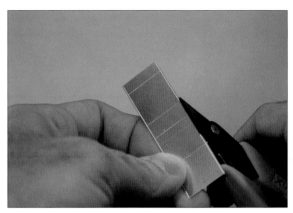

The Xuron photoetch shears are used to cut off the nubs left over on the photoetch piece. They cut the small bits off cleanly without bending the photoetch piece. (JA)

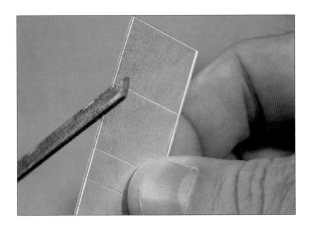

A metal file was used to clean up the edges of the photoetch pieces. I run this along the whole edge to make it smooth throughout. (JA)

The Etch Mate is very handy when trying to bend long pieces of photoetch. The side fenders need their edges bent to 90 degrees, and the long folding blade makes this easy. (JA)

The front fender, as provided by Aber. It has indentations that will need to be pushed out to represent bolts and a ridge, and a line where it will be bent at 90 degrees. (JA)

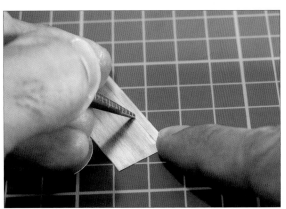

The ridge can be easily pushed in using the Multi Tool. The bolts on the fender were pushed in with a ball-point pen. (JA)

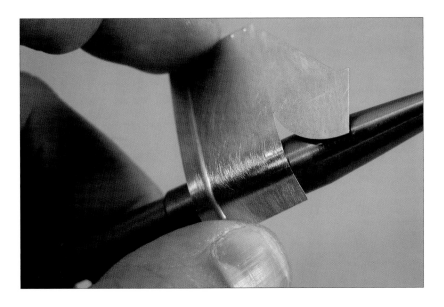

Forming a bend in photoetch using the Multi Tool. This tool features different diameters, allowing you to obtain the correct curve. (JA)

To start the soldering process, the specific photoetch piece needs to be separated from the fret. I use a scalpel for this, and simply push against the small bit joining the piece to the fret until it gives. I do this in a way that gives me some leftover of the bit on the piece, as I do not want to damage the photo-etch piece I am going to use. Then I straighten out the 'nub' with tweezers, snip it off with Xuron photoetch shears, and file the remaining bit clean, if any of it remains. The Xuron shears are very useful, as they snip off the bits cleanly without bending the photoetch at all. To make the photoetch hinges, I use a technique taught to me by my good friend Paul Alderton: I place the two parts of the hinges together with the wire for the hinge in between, all anchored within one of my Etch Mate's spaces. I fold up the arms of the hinges slightly before putting the components together on the Etch Mate. Then it is a simple matter of folding the arms of the hinges over the wire and tucking them in – very quick and easy.

When I am going to solder something, I test-fit first; then I make sure to anchor at least one of the two items I will solder together. Usually I use tape to secure one of the items onto a ceramic tile, which does not conduct heat. The tape is placed away from the area I will solder, but I try to tape down a good portion of the anchored item, as I do not want it shifting about as I work. Next, I shave tiny bits of solder from the little bar of solder, and use the brush from the cap of Tix Flux to place a small amount of flux onto the two I items I wish to join. By placing the flux first, I can then drop shavings of solder onto the area, as the flux is a little sticky. I then pick up the second item of photoetch with tweezers and place it onto the anchored photoetch, in the exact way I want them joined. At that point, I can push the solder shavings in tight to the contact area of the two photoetch pieces with a hobby knife tip, if necessary.

After this setting-up process, I turn on the soldering iron and keep it away from the area I want to solder until it has heated up, which with my Wahl Clipper soldering iron is about five seconds. At that point I place the iron tip onto the area to be sealed, and gently 'melt' the shavings and nudge them into the joint. I do not release the tweezers until a couple of seconds have passed from when I stopped soldering, which allows the join to cool down and seal. I then use a metal file to clean up the area of excess solder. As you can see in the accompanying pictures, it leaves a really clean join.

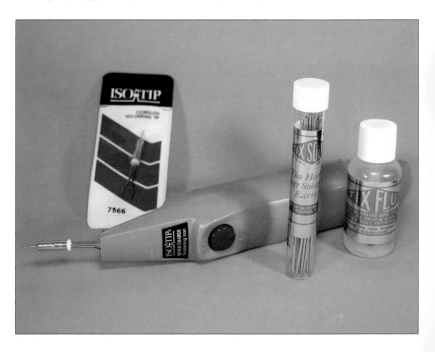

The items I use to solder photoetch: the cordless Iso Tip soldering iron with micro tip, Tix Flux, and Tix Solder. (JA)

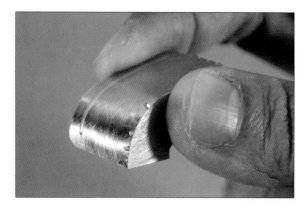

The gap in the fender, where I applied the flux and shavings of solder. I turn on the soldering iron, let it heat up, and then spread the solder along the gap, filling it in. (JA)

The fender after the edge has been soldered. It's quite messy, but the gap has now been filled in. A little work with a metal file and the join will be easily cleaned up. (JA)

The front fender completed, with the previous gap now in pristine condition. It would be very difficult to obtain similar results using CA glue. I actually left the front fenders off the finished model. (JA)

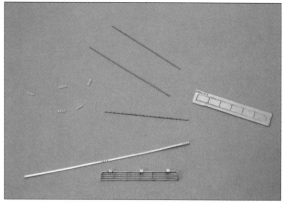

The components used to construct the grilles on the rear hull, along with a completed grille. These are quickly and easily constructed using the soldering iron and tweezers. (JA)

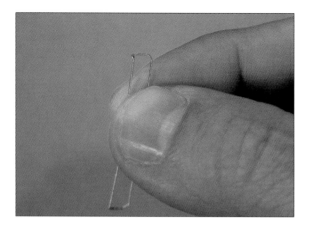

The frame of the grille. The curves of the upper edges were formed using the Multi Tool, and then the open area was soldered shut. (JA)

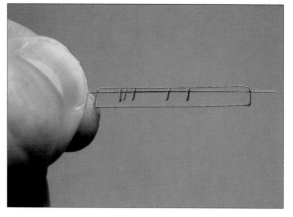

After sealing off the open end of the grille, thread the first wire through, with the struts contained in the inner part by the wire. Then thread the other two wires, passing them through the struts as well. (JA)

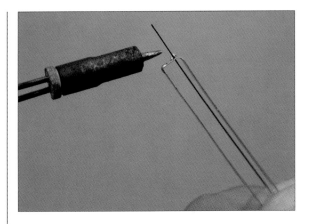

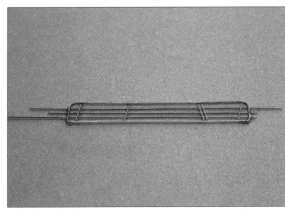

Once the wire is passed through, seal the wire in place by soldering the outer edge/wire. Having done this, you can clip the wire flush to the outer edge and sand off the excess solder. (JA)

Here you see the three wires in place, with the ends soldered. The struts are currently free but now the whole grille can be manipulated for strut placement without it falling apart. (JA)

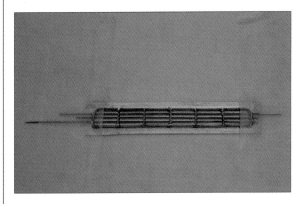

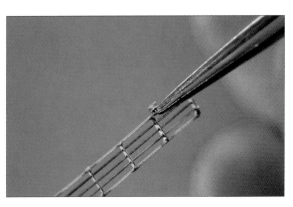

The grille is now secured on the template, and the struts have been placed and soldered (except the middle one). The grille has been taped onto a ceramic tile, which does not conduct heat. (JA)

The last items are the braces that are attached to the hull. I held each one securely in place with tweezers, placed the flux and a small piece of solder on it, then soldered it onto the grille frame. (JA)

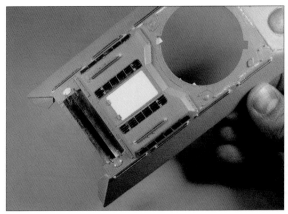

Here is what lies under the grilles, completely soldered together, with plasticard hex nuts. The vent actually rotates freely, as the ends lie within small photoetch brackets that are soldered into place. (JA)

The four grilles in place, with the vent covers underneath them as well. The two vents over the transmission are also in place and need to have their ends sealed over, within a bulge that is part of the hull. (JA)

The Aber transmission cover, soldered together including the latches. The little domed cover at the midline that goes over the rear light was made from brass sheet. (JA)

The underside of the transmission cover shows the extra added detail. The four hinges all work. Once you have practised a little with soldering, making an item like this is not difficult, and well worth the effort. (JA)

The soldered photoetch joint is a great deal stronger than one created with CA glue, and allows much easier manipulation when creating damage. It also helps a modeller when the photoetch has a small join area to hold a heavy item, such as the turret skirt racks on a Panzer IV, for example. It is also possible to solder photoetch to plastic, but this is a bit trickier. To do this, first you place the photoetch flush onto the plastic of the kit (the hull, for example). Then you let the soldering iron heat up as usual, but this time neither flux nor solder are used. You simply bring the tip in perpendicular to the photoetch, and very, very gently push the photoetch into the plastic slightly. I cannot emphasize the 'gently' instruction enough: you only need to push it in a little and it will be joined forever. You can then apply a small amount of liquid plastic model cement to the ridge of plastic around the photoetch and texture it to represent a weld seam. The lower brace of the large rear fuel tanks were attached to the plastic in this manner, and then I glued a plasticard hex nut over it.

The construction phase completed, seen from the starboard side. The Aber straps for the ice cleats are in place, as are the Modelkasten tracks. (JA)

The left side of the completed construction shows the Aber rack for the two-man saw and the photoetch storage box with a bent-up corner. The splash-guard armour on the hull upper edge has two demarcation lines. (JA)

A close-up of the left side showing the storage box detail with grab handles and braces, and the weld seam attaching the fender to the hull. Notice this particular weld seam skips along the edge, and is not continuous. (JA)

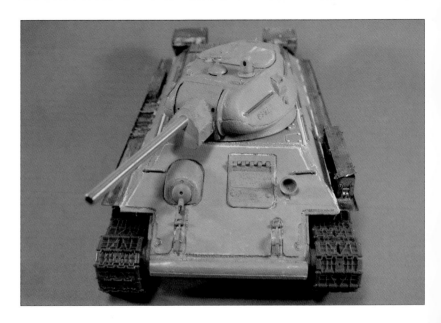

This view shows the difference between the cast steel and rolled steel parts of the tank, the weld seams of the appliqué armour and the 'nose' of the tank, and the casting numbers on the turret. (JA)

This shot of the rear hull shows off the new overlapping rear hull and the Factory 112 specific hinges, the Moskit exhausts, the Aber large rear fuel tanks, the Aber transmission cover and the towing pintle. (JA)

Painting and weathering

The construction process completed, the model was painted and weathered by my friend Mark Neville. He did a fantastic job, as I am sure you can see from the accompanying images. See the photos and captions that follow for details of Mark's techniques and the materials used.

The painted model on a display base. Before applying any colour to a model, I undercoat everything except the tracks in grey aerosol primer, due to the different materials used in construction. (DP)

ABOVE The rear hull of the finished model, painted and weathered by Mark Neville. (DP)

BELOW My choice for the painting was a green colour that would provide a contrast to the dirtier parts of the vehicle. For this I used Vallejo acrylics and shaded the model with very diluted black ink. (DP)

ABOVE The mud and dust were made with designer's gouache mixed with pastel or pigment powders, applied both as a wet wash and in dry form. Pigment powder mixed with acrylic gel gives texture to the mud. (DP)

BELOW Tonal changes in the green were achieved using tinted washes of oil paints, with localized washes of Burnt Umber and Black used to bring out smaller details. (DP)

ABOVE Surface damage was applied using a fine brush or stippled on with a sponge using acrylics or oils. (DP)

BELOW Areas of high wear were highlighted using powdered graphite and various pencils to give a subtle metallic look. (DP)

ABOVE Polish eagle markings were painted by hand using gouache, using references as a guide. These markings were applied by crew members and varied in both quality and shape. (DP)

BELOW A frontal view of the finished model. (DP)

Early T-34/76 Model 1943 'Sniper'

Subject:	*Early T-34/76 Model 1943 'Sniper'*
Modeller/photos:	*Mike Kirchoff*
Skill level:	*Advanced*
Base kits:	*Dragon T-34/76 Model 1941 kit no. 6205*
	Dragon T-34/85 UTZ Model 1944 kit no. 6203
	Tamiya T-34/76 Model 1943 kit no. 35059
Scale:	*1/35*
Additional detailing sets used:	*Trakz Early T-34/76 Interior kit no. TX 0117*
	Miniarm T-34 (UVZ) N. Tagil 1942 Turret kit no. B35024
	Miniarm T-34 Spider web wheels with perforated tyres kit no. B35014
	Modelkasten T-34 Model 1941 tracks kit no. SK-35
	Modelkasten Bolt & Nut Set no. A-1
	CMK T-34 Transmission set kit no. 3006
	Aber T-34 Fenders 35-A45
	Evergreen .010, .015, .020, .030, .040 sheet, strip and rod styrene
	Acorn Enterprises .004, .007, .011, .017, and .026 copper wire

Introduction

While researching another project, I became enamoured with a magnificent series of images taken by photographer Mosin Alexandr, depicting a specific T-34/76 Model 1943 during the very earliest stages of restoration. The armoured rear upper deck of the vehicle had been removed, as had the rear panel and engine, leaving the entire interior exposed. What captivated me about the photographs and subject was not only the unique colouration of the vehicle, but also its remarkable overall condition. So, when the opportunity to contribute to this book presented itself, there was no question in my mind which version of the T-34 I wanted to build.

A brief history

'Sniper', as this tank was named, was produced in mid-1942 at the UralVagonZavod (UVZ) manufacturing facilities, also known as Factory 183. An early T-34/76 Model 1943, this tank featured the new 'Gayka' or hex-nut turret, and is the subject of Mosin's excellent photos. Its fate has been well documented in magazines and several websites since being recovered from a swamp in the summer of 2003 where it had been submerged for nearly 60 years. Immediately upon retrieval, restoration began at Kubinka Tank Museum and by April 2005, 'Sniper' had been returned to running condition.

As no single kit was available to accurately portray 'Sniper', I was left with no choice but to bash together a couple of kits and incorporate a handful of aftermarket accessories. Admittedly, this was at first a daunting task. But the challenge was made easier after my good friend Mark Rethoret offered his extensive knowledge of this weapon. Considered by many an authority on the T-34, Mark compiled a fairly elaborate list of additions, corrections and modifications necessary to bring 'Sniper' to life. These included a redesigned

hull, drive wheel, new road wheel arrangement, smaller sight aperture for the bow machine gun, different headlamp set up and a new pin knocker (a wedge-like device mounted behind each drive wheel used to automatically direct track pins back into place). All these areas were addressed in some fashion.

The 'Sniper' T-34/76 completed. (MK)

Construction
The hull

As a Model 1943, 'Sniper' possessed certain characteristics of both -76 and -85 vehicles. A new glacis plate was incorporated featuring a different driver's hatch arrangement and bow machine-gun bulge. Rather than go to all the trouble involved in grafting a T-34/85 glacis onto the Model 1941 hull, I decided to simply scratchbuild the front plate. Laminating three sheets of .015 styrene brought the glacis to the proper level, and not only allowed me to create a nice channel for an epoxy putty weld bead, but also left a nice hard edge for the glacis, as my reference photos indicated would be correct. I then simply cut away the driver's hatch and machine-gun locations using the kit hull as a guide.

Turning my attention to the interior, I removed the swing arm bosses then laid a new floor with sheet styrene. I added the CMK final drive housings and cut out the forward escape hatch and access plate found mid-hull, as per my reference photos.

Next, I fashioned eight new suspension towers from styrene strip using the Trakz parts as a template. I glued four into position in the fighting compartment, making sure each lined up with the appropriate cover on the upper hull roof. I also added two shorter spring covers in the forwardmost locations at this time. A total of ten stub axles were scratchbuilt and positioned accordingly.

I decided to use the Trakz firewall as a template and create my own. Photos indicated one access panel was closed, another left open, while the two middle panels were removed altogether. I needed to account for this, as well as the absence of an interior ventilator, so it was just as easy to scratchbuild this bulkhead.

According to my references, I needed to add a fuel cell between the starboard pair of forward spring towers. This component, exposed after restorers apparently removed the lower panel, was easily replicated by building a simple five-sided box from styrene and further detailed with .010 sheet styrene.

Using a composite cutting wheel I carefully removed the upper deck, making sure I left enough material on the sides to maintain the proper thickness along the top edge. (MK)

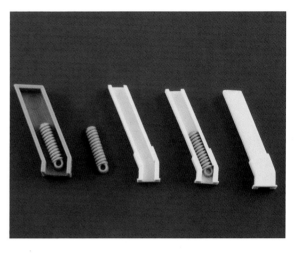

The kit-supplied suspension towers (left) are way overscale. This photo shows the progression I used to scratchbuild the eight suspension towers. (MK)

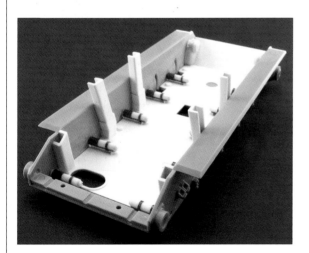

This photo shows work well under way on the lower hull. I've installed a new floor, stub axles, final drives and the forward four suspension towers. Getting each tower to match its access plate on the hull roof was critical, so this was a fairly time-consuming step. The stub axles are cut from 0.10-diameter rod and detailed with lead foil and bolt heads cut from hex rod stock. (MK)

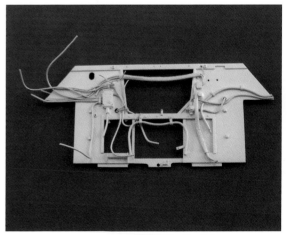

Here is a shot of the aft side of the scratchbuilt firewall. I used the Trakz component as a template to fashion the basic shape from .015 styrene sheet. After cutting away the appropriate panels, I strengthened the assembly with .010 styrene reinforcement strips, and then further detailed it with various gauges of copper, epoxy putty and lead wire and Grandt Line wing nuts. (MK)

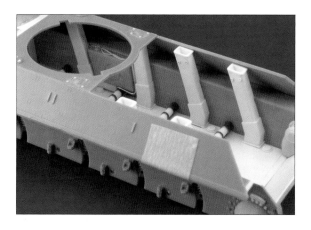

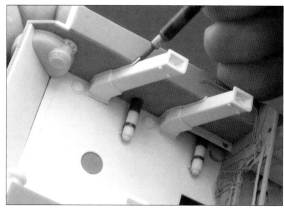

This image shows the rearmost four suspension towers in place. Notice how they coordinate with the upper edge of the armoured side plates. Also visible is the scratchbuilt fuel cell. Once this detail was installed, I added plumbing with both lead wire and epoxy putty, and a quick swipe of Mr. Surfacer 500 (to simulate the rough texture) finished off the detail. (MK)

ABOVE, BELOW LEFT AND RIGHT These three photos show the simple method I use to replicate heavy welds common on vintage armour. First, I roll some epoxy putty into a string about .030in. in diameter. Then, using a brush moistened with water, I place the putty in position. Next, I gently push the putty into the corner, using a rounded-off toothpick to create the 'puddle' effect. After a few minutes I return with the paintbrush to gently smooth out any rough edges. (MK)

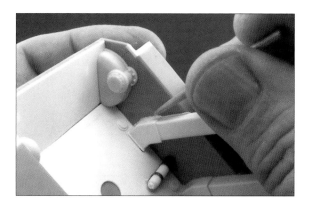

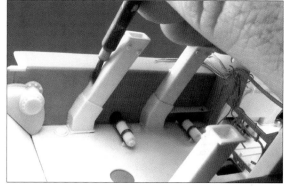

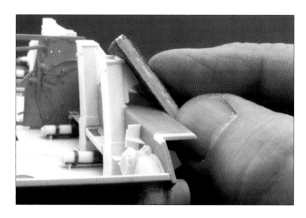

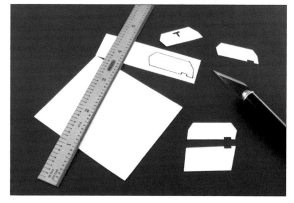

To ensure a good fit with the inner hull sides I intentionally built each suspension tower support oversized, then sanded each down later with a sanding stick. Notice I have already begun detailing both the fighting and engine compartments at this point. (MK)

I started detailing the forward compartment by adding the sheet metal plates that covered the fuel tanks located between the towers. Again, I used the Trakz detail to determine these dimensions. Once cardboard templates were fashioned it was simply a matter of cutting .015 sheet styrene and gluing the parts in place. (MK)

Much patience was required when undertaking all this detailing. I methodically worked my way around the driver's compartment, always having reference photos within easy reach. Here I'm attaching a minute clamp I fashioned from epoxy putty. (MK)

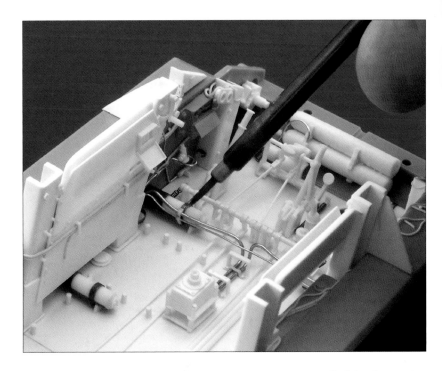

The remaining four suspension towers were now installed in the engine compartment. I found it necessary to test-fit the upper hull to make sure each lined up correctly with the top edge of the side armour. Once I was satisfied with their positioning, they were glued in place. Later, I mixed up some epoxy putty and detailed each tower with simulated welds.

Each tower had a triangular-shaped piece of sheet steel supporting it to the hull sides. The trick is to actually build it a little oversized, then take the edge down with a sanding stick, using the angle created from the top of the suspension tower to the bottom edge of the lower hull.

Even though much of the fighting compartment would be hidden from view after mating the hull halves, I felt compelled to detail it as completely as I could. The open driver's hatch and openings in the firewall still allowed a direct line-of-sight – and you never know who will be peering inside to critique your handiwork!

Following photographs and other reference material, I detailed my way around the forward hull. I managed to put a few Trakz components to good use, including the compressed-air bottle, the driver's steering controls and pedals. Almost everything else was scratchbuilt using sheet and strip styrene, lead, copper and epoxy putty wiring, utilizing fairly simple methods.

Transmission

I couldn't wait to install the terrific CMK transmission. After careful inspection, I found the CMK offering represented a later five-speed transmission and did not exactly correspond to the details found in my reference pics for the four-speed transmission-equipped 'Sniper'. Among the differences were the details residing on the transmission's upper body. I had no choice but to remove and replace them with scratchbuilt versions of my own.

Careful study of my reference photos was time well spent when it came to scratchbuilding the engine stand. It is truly a complex affair – being constructed mostly of angle iron channel and steel plate while being both welded and bolted together. As is my usual practice when attempting to replicate an assembly like this, I first sketched out a fairly detailed rendition of the stand and all its major components.

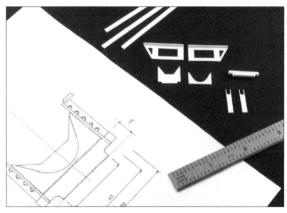

As the CMK offering represented a slightly different transmission I was forced to remove and replace all of the detail on the upper body. I used appropriate sizes of styrene and copper wire to enhance this area, as well as employing a handful of Modelkasten nut/bolt combinations from their A-1 set. Among other details, I also added new brake bands and retainer straps from .005 styrene strip. (MK)

When tackling a complex assembly like the T-34 engine stand I jot down certain dimensions I feel are important, making note of how all the detail parts correlate. Once the drawing is completed it is simply a matter of cutting parts to proper size and assembly. (MK)

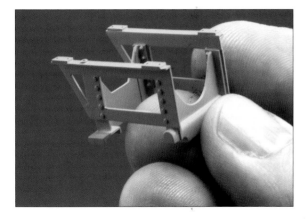

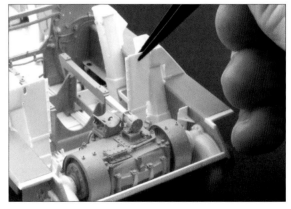

Here is the completed engine stand, resplendent in a coat of Mr. Surfacer 500. Notice how clean the detail looks after priming. (MK)

A steady hand was required when lining up the multiple parts that went into the engine shields. Constructed of .015 styrene, each was further detailed with .010 strip and .020 hex bolts cut from rod stock and given epoxy putty welds. I have also temporarily installed the transmission to ensure I had enough clearance for the shields. (MK)

Once the engine stand was completed, I installed it, along with the transmission. Then, I finished up the rear compartment by adding a pair of scratchbuilt shields.

Painting and weathering the interior

When I was satisfied that all the internal hull details had been addressed to my liking, I airbrushed on two thin primer coats of Mr. Surfacer 500. Almost immediately after this, I sprayed on several coats of a charcoal grey I had mixed up, using Vallejo Model Color acrylics.

The entire interior of the vehicle then received a thin but complete wash of Burnt Umber oils thinned with Turpenoid, a synthetic art-grade turpentine. This step is crucial to the overall effect as it created continuity between the two shades of paint.

Primed and ready for paint. I was really pleased with the results after I airbrushed two coats of Mr. Surfacer 500 on the interior. I diluted the primer with its recommended solvent – Mr. Leveling Thinner. Don't forget to prime the upper hull interior as well. (MK)

I decided to give the interior a charcoal grey base in preparation for its earth tone scheme. This custom colour consisted of six parts Vallejo Model Color Dark Blue Grey (867), three parts Red Leather (818) and a hint of White (951). This was reduced with distilled water at a 4:6 paint-to-thinner ratio. (MK)

I thought it was important to apply a complementary colour to the grey as a first step in weathering the interior. Here I'm using another custom blend, this time a light brown I mixed with six parts English Uniform (70921), and two parts each of Burnt Umber (941) and Yellow Ochre (913). (MK)

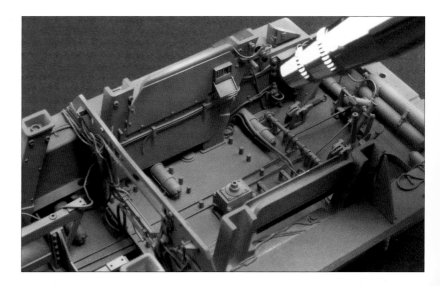

Here is the simple selection of pigments, pastel chalks and thinner I used throughout this project. (MK)

You can see the tremendous latitude the combined use of pigments, pastels and oils affords. Here I'm applying a pin wash – a controlled effect used to accentuate existing details. (MK)

Another excellent photo of the real 'Sniper', this time exposing the interior of the rear compartment. Notice the red primer on the suspension towers and the haphazard accumulation of cables and wiring remaining after the engine was removed. (MA)

This photo of the rear hull taken prior to the installation of the transmission is a good example of how pigments used in conjunction with oils render very realistic results. (MK)

The CMK transmission installed in the rear of 'Sniper'. Its faded-white body stands in stark contrast to the soiled and stained interior. Note how busy the interior looks, even with the engine removed. (MK)

This is the final effort in the driver's compartment. I purposefully left the interior lighter than my references indicated in an attempt to make it easier to notice the details. (MK)

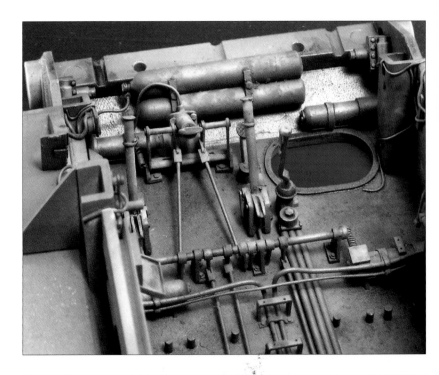

This is a good shot of the aft side of the firewall. Note how natural the plumbing, wiring and cables appear. Also, a bit of red primer was exposed on the suspension towers when restorers removed oil and fuel tanks. I simulated this with a like-coloured pastel chalk. (MK)

Admittedly, I was a little apprehensive with the next phase of weathering the interior. Most war relics have been reduced to little more than rusted hulks. However, 'Sniper' was spared this fate by its lengthy submersion in the swamp. Therefore, the interior of the tank seemed more dirty than rusted, necessitating the use of more earthy tones. Purely by accident, I happened upon a splendid combination of MIG Production pigments and, when thinned with Humbrol Enamel Thinner, was able to achieve the results I was looking for. I further tried to bring the interior to life by using various shades of chalk pastels and artist's oils.

The transmission had quite a unique appearance as the aluminium body had oxidized to the point that it appeared almost white. I simulated this by first

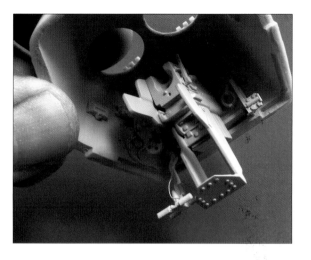

A clear shot of how I managed to install the Trakz breech assembly into the turret. Also note the detail on the inside of the left turret wall and the even coating of Mr. Surfacer 1000 on the interior. (MK)

This is the outstanding Miniarm hex-turret with Trakz F34 breech assembly installed, painted and weathered. Miniarm took great pains to replicate the uneven texture of all external surfaces of the turret. I further distressed these areas with a tiny steel-cutter in my Dremel using the photos found on the website as reference. (MK)

painting the entire transmission with the same custom charcoal grey colour I had used on the interior, then brushed on several layers of nearly translucent Model Color white that had been thinned with distilled water. This allowed some of the darker colour to show, creating a very authentic cloudy effect.

Detailing the turret

The terrific Miniarm T-34 (UVZ) N. Tagil 1942 Gayka (or hex-nut) turret was the only game in town if I wanted to accurately portray 'Sniper'.

I wanted to use as much of the Trakz turret interior as possible, but this meant some adaptation. I managed to incorporate the Trakz F34 breech and

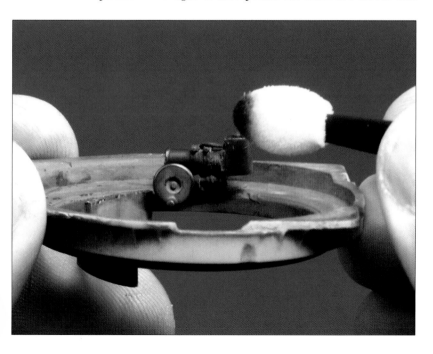

Using a small cosmetic applicator I rubbed a bit of graphite on the turret drive motor. Remember, a little of this effect goes a long way. (MK)

The drive wheel needed a bit of reworking so I carefully ground away the bolted roller details found on the outer surface of each wheel half. Once that tedious task was accomplished I slathered a bit of Mr. Surfacer 500 on the wheel to even things up a bit. (MK)

Here I am adding more primer to all external surfaces of the model, including the tracks. Taking the time to carefully texture all appropriate areas of the model really pays off in the weathering stage. (MK)

guard easily, while I resorted to removing the forward ¼-inch of each trunnion and just glued them to the inside face of the turret – simple enough.

To complete the turret interior, I added a Trakz pistol port to the rear, a junction box to the left side, drive motor to the turret ring, then scratchbuilt a pair of lens boxes for each sidewall. Externally, I used the Miniarm components with the exception of replacing the PTK-5 armoured sight cover with Mark Rethoret's terrific casting and simulating the thin sheet metal rain guard with lead foil.

'Sniper' had a mix of both all-steel and half-spider rubber-tyred road wheels. Also, the drive wheel had some fairly obvious differences when compared with available kit parts. I found the all-steel wheels as a stock offering in Tamiya kits, while Miniarm produces a beautiful set of the half-spider running gear I was looking for.

I had originally intended to scratchbuild the drive wheel, but considering I was pressed for time, I opted to modify the kit parts instead.

I used the exceptional Aber fenders which were installed without a hitch. Using photos as a reference, I used my Dremel to simulate areas that had rusted through on the right fender before gluing them to the hull sides. I then stippled on a light application of Mr. Surfacer 500 around those areas to further accentuate them. This really paid dividends when I began the weathering process later.

Tracks

The final step in construction was the installation of the Modelkasten tracks. Unique to this vehicle, I used the SK-35 workable tracks, and they were a breeze to assemble. Once the tracks were installed, I applied a liberal coating of Mr. Surfacer 500 in order to simulate the cast surface of the links and to give subsequent layers of effects better adhesion.

Painting and weathering

After masking off all hatches and the entire rear opening, I primed the model with Mr. Surfacer 1000 from a spray can in preparation for the first colour coat.

This is 'Sniper' after a complete application of primer. Here all the small details really begin to stand out, such as the scratchbuilt head lamp, tow shackle retaining clips and welds. (MK)

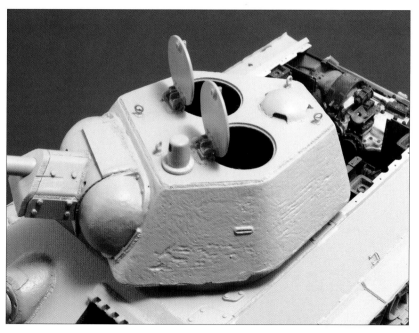

This photo shows the effect of several applications of Mr. Surfacer on the turret. These subtle nuances really make the difference in the finished piece. (MK)

As soon as the primer was dry I airbrushed the ubiquitous charcoal grey colour onto the tracks and lower extremities. It was important to ensure coverage between and behind each road wheel. In doing so, the necessity to paint the rubber tyres on the half-spider road wheels was alleviated.

External paint

Needless to say, I couldn't wait for this phase of the project! As I mentioned earlier, 'Sniper' sported a rather unique colour scheme. From what I can ascertain, the vehicle was originally painted with the typical Soviet Green, and then at some point, a winter whitewash was applied. This was obvious as 'Sniper' still had vestiges of this on the turret, among other areas. A close examination of my reference photos uncovered a remarkable third colour – a light, grey-green that

One of Mosin Alexandr's magnificent images. This shows full well the variance of colour found on 'Sniper'. Notice the remnants of a winter camouflage and the mysterious 'third colour'. (MA)

swirled around the turret, the right rear hull and encompassed the entire left hull side. My conclusion was that the lime-based whitewash had leeched pigment from the overall green over the years, leaving this lighter colour. A quick check of the Vallejo chart proved that Model Color Stone Grey (884) seemed to be the closest match to this off-the-wall shade.

With that in mind I airbrushed the appropriate areas of the model with Vallejo Model Color Russian Green (894), making sure to include the running gear. This was followed by an application of Stone Grey, taking care to match the pattern with my reference images as best I could.

At this point, I applied my now-standard Burnt Umber wash to bring balance to the two camouflage colours. Once completely dry, I began the process of replicating the mottled appearance of the vehicle. Taking a tip from Nicola Cortese's *Modelling IS Heavy Tanks* (Osprey Modelling no. 9), I decided to use the sponge technique to simulate this effect. This method is simple to learn and easy to master. Using a bit of cosmetic sponge, I dabbed thinned Russian Green in a random but controlled pattern around the vehicle. To complement that effect, I also used a neutral grey, but limited its application to just a few strategic locations.

Using a fine-pointed brush, I also added minute dots, streaks and scratches with both green and light green basic camouflage colours. This step worked quite well to contrast the effects I had obtained with the sponge. This treatment was not limited to the hull: the turret received its fair share of attention too.

A scriber was used to lightly scratch the side armour in a few places. I've employed this method in the past and it works wonderfully. By actually compromising the surface, you peel up a small amount of paint. The scratch then readily accepts a diluted rust mixture – in this case thinned Burnt Sienna

I was really pleased with Vallejo's interpretation of Soviet Green. Reduced with distilled water and a few drops of Model Color Thinner (524) this paint airbrushed beautifully. (MK)

Deciding to airbrush straight Stone Grey worked out very well. By the time I had gone through the entire weathering process I was very satisfied with the contrast to the Soviet Green. (MK)

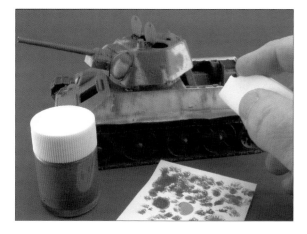

The sponge technique was a breeze to master. Using a cosmetic sponge and thinned Soviet Green paint, I was able to achieve just the effect I was striving for. The trick is to dab most of the paint from the sponge before committing to the model – essentially the same method as dry-brushing. (MK)

A shot of how all the effects employed came together. (MK)

Following my reference photos I brushed a diluted mixture of Model Color White to specific areas of the model to simulate the worn whitewash. I returned to those areas later, applying a few streaks and dots to create more intensity, followed by a light wash of oils. (MK)

oils. When dry, I gently rub off the previously peeled paint, leaving a neat and tidy but rusty scratch.

The next task at hand was the creation of a winter camouflage scheme. I covered the appropriate areas with diluted Model Color White, allowing the light green base to show through occasionally. A random pattern of white dots was then applied, followed up with a brief wash of Burnt Umber again, to help bring all the colours together on a common plane.

Markings and weathering

At the time of recovery, this tank sported few discernible markings. The name 'Sniper' was to be painted in Cyrillic on each turret side, just above the vision

This particular vehicle had few obvious markings, but close examination revealed the numerals '918-6' and the Cyrillic spelling of 'Sniper' on both sides of the turret. (MK)

The results achieved with the full battery of pigments. This product was easy to use, very forgiving and yielded just the effect I was hoping for. (MK)

slits. The number '918-6' was painted in white on the right turret side while a black number '70' was found forward of the aerial on the right hull side.

Reference photos of 'Sniper' indicated a full complement of mud and grass packed into the tracks, over the running gear and underside of the hull. I was anxious to simulate this with pigments. I approached this in three stages. The first step was a light washing of MIG Productions' European Dust diluted with enamel thinner over all the above-mentioned areas and the extreme lower hull and glacis. I took special care to reach all the areas behind the running gear, including the undersides of the fenders. I then added more pigment to my mix, along with short clippings of scale grasses and a small amount of Durham's Water Putty, creating a mud-like consistency. I concentrated this on the tracks,

Another view of 'Sniper' showcasing the different effects. (MK)

This photo demonstrates the very realistic rust effects that are possible with pigments. Notice the contrast to the Soviet Green, the subtle changes in shades and the simple 'palette' I use. (MK)

road wheels and behind the idler and drive wheels. While still moist, I doused these areas with dry pigments.

To finish off the tracks, I rubbed pigment from the raised cleats and then lightly burnished those areas with graphite. Pin washes of several colours were then applied to the mud effects around the vehicle – just to add a bit of character.

The final touch for this model involved adding rust effects. I decided to address the fenders initially and began by applying a slurry of European Dust pigment diluted with enamel thinner onto each fender. The right-side fender received a bit more attention, concentrating the pigment around the worn-through areas. This acted as a highlight for the other shades of rust about to be used. When dry, I stippled Burnt Sienna oils in basically the same areas as the pigment. I then followed this up with both Standard and Light Rust pigments, taking advantage of the rough texture caused by the Mr. Surfacer 500 I had applied previously, and came away with some very interesting effects.

When satisfied with these results I then methodically worked my way around the vehicle, adding hints of rust to details such as tow shackles, hinges and welds.

Summary

Building this model was quite an experience. Employing terrific kits and after-market accessories, along with outstanding reference material and expert advice, made it extremely enjoyable. Even the intense scratchbuilding is well within the talent and means of most skill levels – it is merely a matter of preparation and planning, in conjunction with fundamentally sound methods.

BELOW, OPPOSITE AND NEXT PAGE **The finished model. (MK)**

STZ T-34/76, Italian Army

Subject:	Stalingrad Tractor Plant (STZ) T-34 in use with the Italian Army
Modeller/photos:	Adam Wilder
Skill level:	Advanced
Base kit:	DML early T-34/76 Model 1941
Scale:	1/35
Additional detailing sets used:	MIG Productions STZ T-34 conversion set Eduard photoetch parts On-The-Mark Models photoetch set Bronekater Bk 1125 Turret, MIG Productions model Friulmodel workable metal tracks
Special references:	Guglielmi, D. – interview via e-mail

Introduction

When I started modelling 15 years ago my primary subjects of interest were 'Germans and Shermans'. As a result of growing up in America, I was much more educated and familiar with the Normandy and African campaigns of World War II.

One day my local hobby shop received a new shipment of Tamiya models. Among the boxes were kits of both the SU-85 and SU-122 Russian self-propelled guns. Up to this point I had never even heard of these T-34 variants. The SU-122 reminded me of a wild boar and I immediately purchased both of the models.

While building these models I started researching the T-34. Of course I also started learning more about the German–Russian campaign waged during World War II. I found the numbers of both the men and material involved in this conflict staggering, notably at battles such as Kursk and Stalingrad.

I also started to develop a keen interest in the Russian Army, about which I knew so little. I was surprised to find that the Russians had been able to both engineer and produce, in large quantities, excellent weapons such as the PPSH Tommy gun, T-34 battle tank, and Mig fighter airplane. In spite of these, the T-34 continued to capture my interest. Like the American Sherman tank, the T-34 was produced in enormous numbers, was used by numerous countries, and was the base for a number of fascinating variants.

The T-34 was cheap to manufacture; could be produced quickly; and was simple to maintain, reliable and moderately easy to operate – again, much like the American Sherman. Its wide tracks, torsion-bar suspension, sloped armour and diesel engine actually appear to have made it a better weapon than the Sherman. Its shape and low silhouette made the T-34 much more attractive and interesting to me than the Sherman and Tiger tanks I had already spent so much time modelling.

To date, I have spent most of my hobby time modelling the Russian T-34 battle tank and its variants. The numerous camouflages, markings and alterations continue to capture my interest. The Stalingrad Tractor Plant (STZ) model is the one T-34 that has always been the most interesting for me.

In this chapter I will focus primarily on the major steps needed to convert one of the DML early T-34/76 Model 1941 kits into a slightly later STZ variant. The steps and techniques shown will primarily focus on using the sheet-plastic,

The T-34/76 in Italian service. (AW)

glues and abrasive tools needed to easily complete this conversion. The second part of this chapter will look at painting and weathering a captured STZ T-34 in use by the Italian Army.

The Stalingrad Tractor Plant T-34s – a brief history

The Stalingrad Tractor Plant is said to have manufactured T-34/76 tanks until September 1942, when the Germans reached the fringes of the city. There are unconfirmed rumours of T-34 tanks being produced and sent straight into battle without paint or gun-sighting instruments.

The T-34/76 tanks produced at the Stalingrad Tractor Plant during 1942 had some unique details that distinguished them from the other T-34/76s manufactured throughout Russia. These details include the infamous interlocking hull plates that have discouraged enthusiasts from constructing more models of this variant. Another distinct feature of the STZ T-34/76 is the hatchet-shaped housing protecting the 76mm gun, which was produced close by at the Barrikady plant.

The STZ T-34 that I constructed for this chapter has the more common welded turret containing the simplified undercuts beneath the gun. There were also T-34s produced at the Stalingrad Tractor Plant which were equipped with a less common two-part cast turret. I have also observed photos and drawings of STZ T-34s with 'hooks' on the sides of the hull to fasten the earlier style external rectangular fuel cells.

Construction

I decided to use the recent DML German Army T-34/76 kit as the base for the STZ T-34 in this chapter. This T-34 kit is actually a 1941 variant with some extras such as a German cupola, tools and hull stowage boxes. The T-34/76 Model 41 had some details that differ from the STZ production types but the overall dimensions and features of the hull are generally the same.

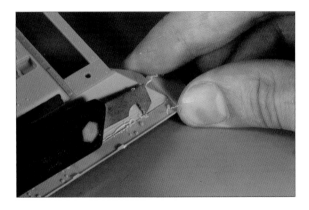

Removing the fenders: making a rough cut with a razor. (AW)

The fenders are then bent and detached from the hull. (AW)

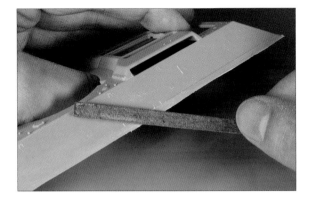

Using a file to remove the excess parts of the fender. (AW)

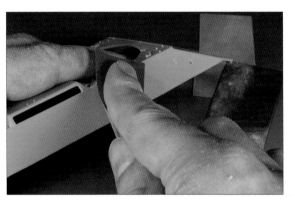

Three different grades of sandpaper were used to ensure a smooth finish on the hull. (AW)

When constructing a model such as the T-34 I recommend that you start by removing large parts such as the fenders if you are planning to add photoetch brass replacements. It is easier to remove these larger parts before other fragile pieces are added. After making a rough cut with a razor, I removed the excess parts of the fender using a file. Three different types of sandpaper were used to ensure a smooth finish on the hull that would not interfere with the appearance of the model's finish. First start with a rough grit sandpaper, then use the medium and finish with the finest.

After removing the fenders I needed to do some more work to the hull before adding the fine details. The discouraging areas of the STZ T-34s for most modellers are the interlocking hull plates. If I am not mistaken, none of the T-34 kits on the market at the time of writing have the interlocking type plates. Although time-consuming, these interlocking areas are not too difficult to recreate.

On this STZ T-34, I first found a good reference to help me get an accurate idea as to the dimensions of the dovetails that interlock the plates. I found some nice 1/35-scale drawings in a book called *T-34 Mityczna Bron*, Vol. I from Armagedon. The drawings in this book are to 1/35 scale so no mathematical skills are necessary. I marked the plates then filed away the ends where the plates would interlock. I made a straight line to aid me in removing the proper amount of the rear plate. It is important that you do not remove too much or too little to ensure that the front and rear plates sit properly in their places in relation to the upper and lower hull.

I ended up scratchbuilding the entire front upper hull plate (more on this shortly). However, first some minor adjustments needed to be made to the

The 1/35-scale drawings in *T-34 Mityczna Bron*, Vol. I from Armagedon provided very useful reference for the interlocking plates. (AW)

I drew a straight line to aid me in removing the proper amount of the rear plate. (AW)

To bond the parts I used Flash superglue and the Insta-Set accelerator. (AW)

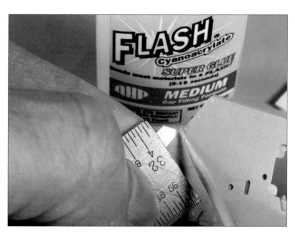

After supergluing the part in place with the aid of a straight edge, apply a bit of the Insta-Set over the adhesive with a toothpick. (AW)

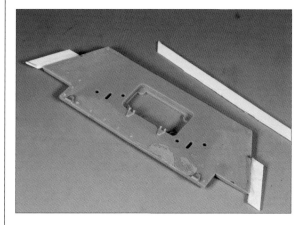

The sheet-plastic firmly glued in place, ready for sanding. (AW)

Sanding the front of the plate where the parts are joined with a flat piece of sandpaper, as shown here, avoids the need for putty to fill the gaps. (AW)

upper rear plate. Pieces of sheet plastic needed to be superglued to the sides of the rear plate to make the dovetails that would interlock it with the sides.

To construct the dovetails I used superglue in conjunction with a product called Insta-Set from Mark Twain Hobby Center. The Insta-Set will greatly speed up the drying of the superglue, significantly reducing the time needed for you to hold the parts together. Superglue the part in place with the aid of a straight edge then apply a bit of the Insta-Set over the adhesive with a toothpick. The superglue will dry almost instantly.

After firmly gluing the sheet-plastic you can sand the dovetails down to their appropriate dimensions. If you carefully sand the front of the plate where the parts are joined with a flat piece of sandpaper, no putty will be needed to fill the gaps. Attaching the dovetails in this manner instead of with plastic cement and putty will save you about 24 hours' work and result in a better appearance.

After completing the dovetails on the upper rear plate I needed to add a few more details. The bolt pattern on the rear plate was removed and updated. The lower rear plate was also updated. To update the lower rear plate you will need to remove the Model 1941-style cable mounts and add the later style. The resin replacements used are from the MIG Productions STZ T-34 conversion set. New welds were added around the gear housings – of which more in a little while.

The upper front plate was a bit more complicated, but not too difficult. As I mentioned earlier, I decided to scratchbuild the entire part. I chose to do this because the DML T-34/76 models are all early variants with the Model-1940-style front hatch. The earlier-style cable mounts were also present on the front of the model. These details, coupled with the hatch and the dovetails that I needed to add, persuaded me to simply rebuild the entire part.

There are dovetails on the lower part of the upper front plate where the lower hull sides connect. These dovetails are hidden when the front fenders are attached. The three photos I referenced for this particular Italian T-34 showed the front fenders to be missing. The line drawings of the hull inside the *T-34 Mityczna Bron* book clearly show these dovetails.

After notching the front parts of the lower hull plates I stated constructing the new upper plate. You will need a protractor to properly transfer the angles from the hull of the DML kit onto the sheet-plastic. Start with a centreline and work all of your dimensions from the middle of the part to ensure symmetry. Use the dovetails on the lower hull plates to help you mark the new part, ensuring a proper fit. The dovetails for the upper side hull plates were added to the fronts of the side plates in the same manner as the rear using superglue and Insta-Set. After gluing on oversized pieces of sheet plastic I again filed them down to the proper size.

Resin accessories from the MIG Productions conversion were added to the front of the hull once it had been attached. The brass piece on the front of the machine-gun housing was taken from an old On-The-Mark Models photoetch set. The welds had to be simulated on the replacement front hull. I used stretched sprue attached with liquid plastic cement to replicate these details. The plastic cement will soften the sprue for a short amount of time allowing you to texture it with a knife.

The bolt pattern on the front lower hull plate needed to be updated. Remove only the lower line of bolts with a knife and sand the surface smooth with fine sandpaper.

I also carried out some other work needed to construct an STZ T-34 variant. The top plate where the turret sits also interlocks with the side plates on the STZ T-34s. I added these dovetails using strips of sheet plastic. The brass fenders and toolboxes are from a couple of Aber sets designed for the DML T-34s. One tip I would like to mention is that it is sometimes easier to glue or solder the finer pieces onto the larger parts on these intricate photoetch sets before forming them.

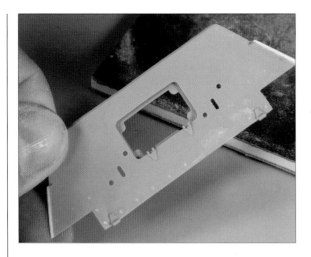

The sanding of the dovetails completed. (AW)

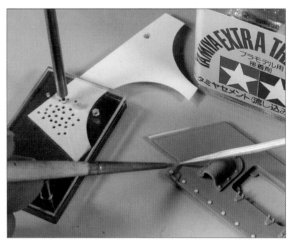

Updating the bolt pattern on the rear plate. (AW)

The Model-1941-style cable mounts were removed on the lower rear plate, and later-style resin replacements were added from the MIG Productions STZ T-34 conversion set. (AW)

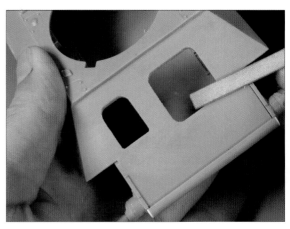

Notching the front parts of the lower hull plates to accept the new, scratchbuilt upper plate. (AW)

Using a protractor to properly transfer the angles from the hull of the DML kit onto the sheet plastic. (AW)

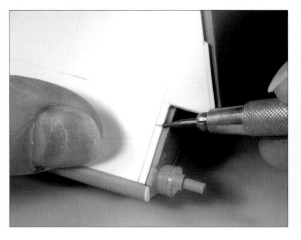

Use the dovetails on the lower hull plates when marking the scratchbuilt part. (AW)

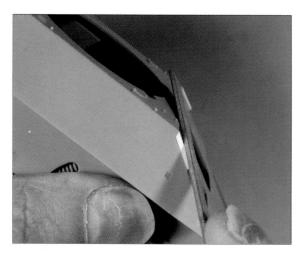

Having added the dovetails for the upper side hull plates, these were filed down to the proper size. (AW)

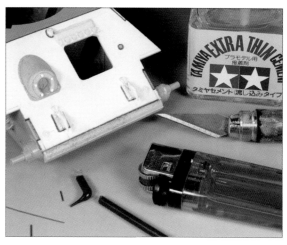

The new front plate attached to the front of the hull, with resin accessories. (AW)

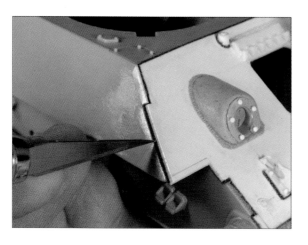

Stretched sprue was glued to the weld seams with plastic cement, and then textured with a knife. (AW)

The bolt pattern on the front lower hull plate was also updated. (AW)

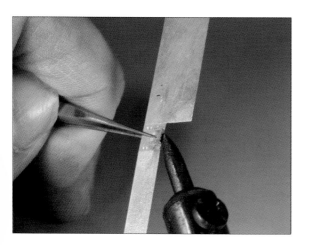

It is easier to attach the finer pieces onto the larger parts of photoetch sets before forming them. (AW)

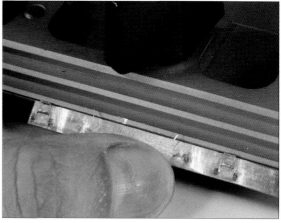

Forming the required angle on the photoetch set with the finer parts attached. (AW)

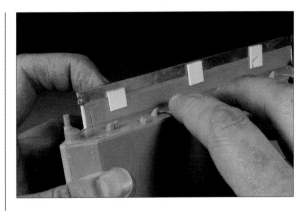

Gluing pieces of thick sheet plastic under the hull can help you when attaching the brass fenders. (AW)

The front of the model with construction phase completed. (AW)

A rear view of the completed construction. (AW)

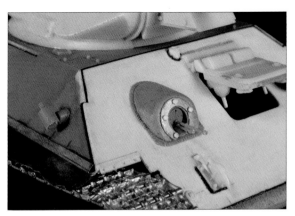

A close-up of the front hull area and machine gun. (AW)

Another key trick is to temporarily glue little pieces of thick sheet-plastic under the hull to aid you in gluing the brass fenders to the model. After the superglue has set, simply remove the plastic parts and discard them.

The rest of the STZ T-34/76 assembly was easy. The turret is an extra Bronekater Bk 1125 turret used on the large resin MIG Productions model. The louvres are also from the MIG Productions STZ conversion kit. The aluminium gun barrel was provided with the DML kit. The Tamiya steel wheels were also used. The Tamiya rubber hubs fit perfectly onto the DML torsion bars. A fine set of workable metal Friulmodel tracks were the final touch.

Creating the tarps

The photos I observed of the Italian STZ T-34 replicated in this article show it covered with tarps. I thought that these tarps would give the model an original appearance. I needed to make and shape the tarps to the model before painting it. Forming the tarps on the model after it was finished might affect the paint job. I made the tarps using a two-part epoxy called Apoxie Sculpt.

I first applied baby (talcum) powder over the model using a mascara brush. The powder prevents the Apoxie Sculpt from sticking to the plastic. I rolled flat sections of Apoxie Sculpt using a flat surface and beer bottle covered with the powder. After rolling the two-part epoxy, I cut the pieces square and applied them randomly over the model. Waves caused by the wind were made to the tarps using paintbrushes. The waves would help to add a feeling of movement to the completed model.

Making the tarps using two-part epoxy – and the reference photo showing their placement. (AW)

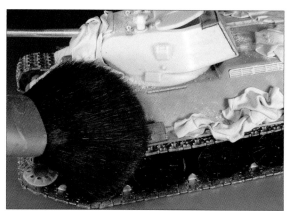

First I applied talcum powder over the model with a cosmetics brush. (AW)

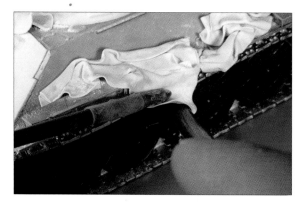

Waves caused by the wind were made using paintbrushes. (AW)

The completed tarps, applied over the model. (AW)

I had to let the Apoxie Sculpt set for a day before carefully removing the tarps from the model. Leaving the tarps in place and painting the piece as a whole might be an option to many modellers. I chose to remove them as I felt it would be easier to paint them separately. I recommend you do what you think is best when painting models featuring such items. At this time I also removed the running gear. Painting the running gear separately would allow me to easily weather beneath the fenders. Painting the tracks separately would permit me to weather them more realistically.

Painting the STZ T-34/76

When asked to contribute to this book, I was at first hesitant, because I could not remember seeing many, or any, STZ T-34s with interesting camouflage schemes, markings or slogans. I did not simply want to construct another green T-34/76. After some quick searching I found a coloured illustration by Peter Sarson in the Osprey New Vanguard No. 9 book *T-34/76 Medium Tank 1941–45* written by Steve Zaloga. The illustration shows a STZ T-34 captured and in use with the Italian Army around Stalingrad. I remembered looking at this image years earlier when the book was first published and wanting to construct this particular STZ T-34, simply for its unique history.

The Italians conquered the central sector of the Eastern Front, together with German and Rumanian troops. From the end of 1942 they protected a long sector on the Don River, north of Stalingrad. The Italians retreated from this sector in January 1943.

The Italian Army captured around 15 Soviet tanks on the Eastern Front. Some of these were obviously T-34s, and one of these was captured by the Germans, then relocated to Italy and tested. The captured T-34 influenced the Italian P 26 heavy tank that was later named the P 40 tank. The T-34 featured in this project was captured in working condition in August 1942. The tank was then put back into use by the HQ of the Italian 53rd Group of the 120th Artillery Regiment of the 3rd Mobile Division.

Although in service with the Italian army, this T-34 still featured a typical overall green finish; however, it retained a few unique aspects. Among these were the numerous large white identification Savoy crosses painted on the tank by its Italian owners. The Cross of Savoy (*Croce di Savoia*) identified the Savoy royal family, and was the sign used on some Italian military vehicles. Another key detail was the numerous tarps placed on the vehicle, for which reasons I am not sure.

The base coats

When painting a model I always start with a simple base coat of Vallejo acrylic paints. Acrylic paints are easy to spray and less toxic than enamels. Acrylic paints also stand up well to the oil and enamel thinners that I use during the weathering steps. I seldom post- or pre-shade a base coat. These same effects can be achieved more realistically with filters, washes and earth colours.

After applying the base coat I apply three coats of gloss onto the entire model. The coats of gloss will further protect the base coat from the weathering steps. The gloss coats will also work in conjunction with the weathering steps to achieve a look of painted steel on the model.

After the gloss coats, I apply a few filters onto the model. Filters will help tone down the gloss while subtly giving a bit of depth to the base coat. Filters will also help to unify a camouflage pattern, if present on the model. Give a filter about two hours to dry.

I applied and blended artist oils onto the model to enrich the base colour and add subtly different tones to each detail. Adding different hues to the details will help to differentiate each part from another, making the model more interesting. Blend the oils using a round paintbrush dampened (not soaked) with turpentine, using downward strokes on the angled and vertical parts and a tapping motion on the horizontal areas such as the top of the hull and turret.

Adding chipped paint can be a lengthy step but it is an important one. It adds a lot of life and realism to a model if done thoughtfully and carefully. I think a good chipped paint job will give a model more of a used metallic appearance than any other weathering step. If you have a new and fine high-quality paint brush, achieving an effective appearance of chipped paint over your model is not difficult.

Spraying on the base coat of Vallejo acrylic paints. (AW)   Applying one of three coats of gloss onto the model. (AW)

Applying the filter coat onto the model. (AW)

Adding artist's oils to the model to enrich the colour. I added more blue oils to the hatch to make it darker once the oils were blended. (AW)

The first step of adding chipped paint: I apply lighter areas of green onto the model where paint chips might occur. (AW)

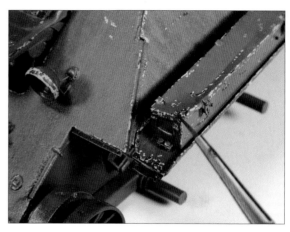

The next step is to add areas of metallic acrylic paints over some of the chips. (AW)

For the rust, I mix a number of different coloured pigments, enamels and oils to achieve different shades. (AW)

Next I apply the various shades of rust over the chips. (AW)

Applying a wash over the entire model. (AW)

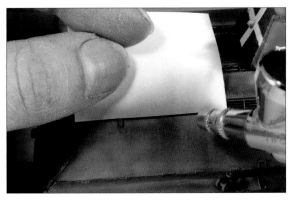

Applying the earth tones onto the model. Here I am using a piece of paper while dusting one part to keep the other parts clean. (AW)

To start, I apply lighter areas of green onto the model where paint chips might occur. These areas represent chipped and polished areas of fresh paint recently exposed to the elements. The satin finish of the lighter green chips will contrast nicely with the glossier finish on the rest of the vehicle. I focus more on the sheet metal parts such as the fenders and tool boxes as well as on the corners of the larger ingots.

For the next step I add areas of metallic acrylic paints over some of the chips. Adding rust is the third step; I mix a number of different coloured pigments, enamels and oils to realistically achieve the different shades of rust that occur on vehicles. I apply the various shades of rust over most of the light-green chips and some of the metallic coloured chips as well.

Next, I added a number of washes over the entire model. The washes add fake shadows, emphasize seams and highlight details. I mix my washes using Humbrol brown enamel paints, Burnt Umber artist oils and turpentine. I mix the enamels, oil paint and turpentine in different ratios depending on the area of the model where I am applying the wash. You will figure out your own techniques for applying washes as you become more comfortable with this step.

Adding the earth tones

After letting both the rust-coloured chips and washes dry for a day, I was ready to start adding the earth tones. I started applying the earth tones onto the model by airbrushing a subtle dusting mixed from Tamiya acrylics. Randomly airbrush the acrylics onto the areas that you want to contain larger amounts of dust. I would recommend areas like around and on the fenders, on the upper hull around the turret and on top of the turret. Review photos of actual tanks to see where dust will collect. You will also want to apply a good coat to the lower hull under the fenders and on running gear as well. This step will work as a base for the rest of the weathering steps.

You can also use this step to help distinguish different components on the model. Use a piece of paper while dusting one part to keep the other parts clean. The matt paint used during this important step will also give the pigments in the upcoming step a coarse surface to adhere to.

Acrylics also help you get subtle and to-scale rain marks on a model. This is another important step that I use in conjunction with the light coats of dust airbrushed in the previous step. Mix a few drops of Tamiya Buff with tap water in a small container such as a plastic medicine cup.

After mixing the water with the acrylic paint, start brushing the nearly clear liquid onto one part of the model at a time using vertical strokes. Keep applying the strokes until the water is dry. As the water dries you will start to see light runs of buff that resemble rain marks of dust. You will need to repeat this step three to four times in one area to get the proper result. Keep this process a random one, applying more runs on some parts of the tank and less on others. Notice that I focused the rain marks on the heavy areas of dust. Also note how the light buff contrasts with the greyer areas airbrushed in the previous step, making this process more noticeable.

With a good base on the model for the earth tones, I was ready to apply the areas of dry mud. I mixed the dry mud for this model using Tamiya Buff along with Dark Mud and Copper Rust pigments. Plaster was also added to the mixture for texture. I applied a good coat on the lower hull beneath the fenders and also onto the running gear. I applied this more sparingly to the upper parts of the hull where the mud might not collect as extensively. Use an old, round paintbrush for this step. These areas on the upper hull were mostly on the rear and front of the model over where the tracks would be.

I have observed in numerous photos of T-34 tanks that large amounts of mud will be thrown up by the track and collect on the rear of the upper hull if the back fenders are missing. I was able to simulate this effect by dipping my brush into the mixture of dry mud and very carefully blowing it onto the rear areas of the hull using my airbrush. Applying mud onto the hull in this manner is very effective. However, you should practise on a piece of scrap paper or on an old model first. You will cover your whole model with splattered mud if you are not careful.

For the next step I added various earth-coloured pigments to the upper hull and running gear using an old and dry brush. Note how I added different tones of pigments in certain areas. Applying different coloured pigments in this manner will help to further differentiate details, like the artist oils discussed previously.

After applying the pigments, I carefully blended them with enamel thinner using a tapping motion with the brush. After this step you will have the base coat of dust working with the lighter dust rain marks and pigments, resulting in a realistic coat of various-toned dust. Next we need to add more fresh mud.

I mixed the fresh mud starting with Humbrol Chocolate then added Dark Mud and Copper Rust pigments. Once again, plaster was added for texture. This time gloss varnish for oil mediums was also implemented.

Using an old brush, I applied the fresh mud mixture to the lower part of the chassis around the torsion bars and randomly over the running gear. After brushing the fresh mud onto an area, I would blend it using enamel thinner or turpentine. Fresh mud was also sprayed onto the rear of the hull using my airbrush.

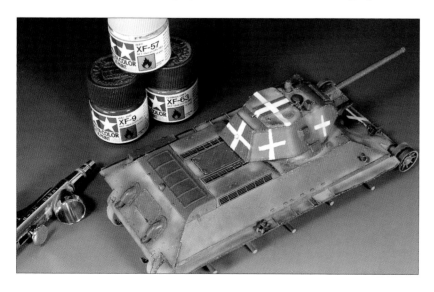

The model after the dusting stage. Compare the areas of dust here to the mud and heavy dust on the completed model. (AW)

I again made a fresh mud mixture using the same ingredients and this time omitted the plaster. I applied the new fresh mud mixture over the upper parts of the hull and fenders using a smaller brush. After brushing the fresh mud onto the upper hull, I again carefully blended it using enamel thinner. This step concluded the application of the earth tones on the T-34. Now I was ready to finish and re-attach the running rear.

Humbrol Aluminum and Gun Metal enamel paints were mixed together and drybrushed onto the outer parts of the steel road wheels. Graphite from a pencil was then rubbed onto the metallic paint using my finger.

The tracks were weathered in the same manner as the rest of the T-34. I started with an airbrushed base coat of Tamiya Dark Earth then applied the dry mud. Finally the fresh mud was brushed on and blended with turpentine. The outer parts of the track were polished using sandpaper. The inner parts of the track were rubbed with a large artist pencil then blended with a rubber-tipped artist tool.

The final touch was to add areas of moisture over the hull and grease around the hubs of the road wheels – another effect that helps make the model more interesting. I performed this step using gloss, satin and matt varnish acrylic paints. I started by applying the gloss and finished with the matt varnish.

Adding rain marks, using a few drops of Tamiya Buff mixed with tap water: use vertical strokes in a random fashion, let them dry, and repeat this step three to four times. (AW)

Notice how I focused the rain marks on the heavy areas of dust. (AW)

Applying the dry mud: a good coat was added to the lower hull beneath the fenders and also onto the running gear. (AW)

The splatter effect – dip your brush into the dry mud mix and carefully blow it onto the rear areas of the hull using an airbrush. (AW)

Next I added earth-coloured pigments to the upper hull and running gear. Note the different tones of pigments used. (AW)

Blending the earth-coloured pigments with enamel thinner. (AW)

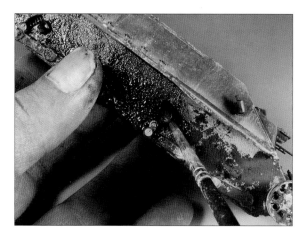

Having applied the fresh mud mixture to the lower part of the chassis, it is blended using enamel thinner or turpentine. (AW)

Fresh mud was also sprayed onto the rear of the hull using my airbrush. (AW)

After brushing the fresh mud onto the upper hull, I carefully blended it using enamel thinner. (AW)

Humbrol Aluminum and Gun Metal enamel paints were mixed together and drybrushed onto the outer parts of the steel road wheels. (AW)

Graphite from a pencil was then rubbed onto the metallic paint using my finger. (AW)

Having weathered the tracks, the outer parts were polished using sandpaper. (AW)

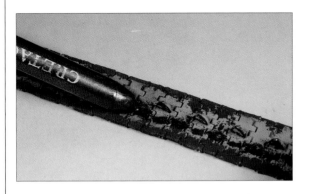

The inner parts of the track were rubbed with a large artist pencil then blended with a rubber-tipped artist tool. (AW)

Adding areas of moisture over the hull using gloss, satin and matt varnish acrylic paints. In this photo, the satin and matt varnishes have not been applied yet, only the gloss. (AW)

The large amounts of dust on a vehicle such as this example will absorb the water quickly. This absorption of the water will result in areas of satin and glossy finishes where moisture is present. Also note how the gloss was added to the corners around the fenders where moisture would collect.

Enamel gloss was mixed with rust-coloured pigments and thinner to make grease. Add more black enamels to make older grease. Apply the grease around the hubs of the road wheels and where it might be present on the upper hull.

The tarps and flags

With the model weathered I then painted the tarps with various coats of grey Vallejo acrylic paints. Shadows and lighter tones of grey were applied with an airbrush. After painting the tarps they were placed back onto the model and weathered. The two flags were made from copper that was primed then painted with acrylics.

Summary

The most time-consuming part of this project was converting the DML T-34 Model 1941 to a 1942 STZ variant. The numerous weathering steps were in essence quite straightforward. Modellers have told me in recent years that, at first, they were afraid to apply these weathering techniques to their well-assembled and painted models. However, after they swallowed their fear and applied the finishing techniques described in this article, they told me they were very happy with what they had achieved. I recommend that you try at least some of the techniques discussed in this article on your next model. Trust me, you will not regret it.

THIS PAGE AND OPPOSITE The finished model, with the tarps and Italian flags added. (AW)

German T-34/76 747(r)-3, Western Front, 1944

Subject:	*T-34/76 747(r)-3, German Army, Western Front, 1944*
Modeller/photos:	*Mig Jimenez*
Skill level:	*Advanced*
Base kits:	*Dragon T-34/76 Model 1941 (Kit No. 6205); T-34/85 UTZ Model 1944 (Kit No. 6203)*
Scale:	*1/35*
Additional detailing sets used:	*Resin turret from TWS Turret roof from Tamiya T-34/76 Model 1943 PART T-34 photoetch*

Introduction

The T-34 provides an endless source of inspiration for many modellers. Although Russian, Polish, Finnish and Czech variants abound, the German versions are some of the most interesting and attractive. The possibility of decorating a T-34 in the colours of the German Army adds a whole new dimension to modelling this fascinating tank. The German Army captured thousands of Soviet vehicles intact and many of them were converted or adapted to improve their performance in combat. This is perhaps the most interesting point for modellers. The conversions carried out to many of these tanks ranged from the addition of simple accessories to transformation into totally different tanks.

The most common and simple modification comprised a simple camouflage scheme or colour change – invariably accompanied by the addition of large German crosses onto the sides of the vehicle. Because the silhouette of the T-34 was easy to spot even at great distances, the crosses were considered vital in determining whether the tank was friend or foe, although they did not always successfully do so.

The next most common modification was the (r)-1 conversion, in which the Germans added small accessories to improve the quality of these tanks. The addition of NOTEK lamps, lateral boxes and the inclusion in some models of a Panzer IV cupola were the most significant improvements. The original T-34/76 did not possess a cupola, and it only had a crew of four men – meaning the tank commander had to act as a gunner too, distracting him from keeping on top of the combat situation. This was one of the reasons why the T-34 was considered inferior to the German Panzer IV in the opening stages of the war. The German Panzer IV had a crew of five, and the commander could focus on directing combat operations from the cupola and its vision blocks. For this reason, the Germans decided to add the cupola to captured T-34s. Later, the Russians saw the light and added their own cupola version to the T-34/76, a feature retained on the new three-man turreted T-34/85 post-1944.

The subsequent modifications to T-34s captured by the Germans were given the (r)-2 and (r)-3 denominations. The (r)-2 had lateral boxes, NOTEK lamps and additional side armour to protect the lower part of the chassis. The (r)-3 was the more advanced conversion, featuring thicker side armour and a Schurzen-style rail around the turret. Few pictures of this rare beast exist.

At the beginning of the war, the Germans tried to modify the T-34 in the field using resources to hand. However, the increase in the numbers of captured vehicles forced the army to send these tanks to the rear for refitting, to cities and locations such as Riga, Görlizt and even the Mercedes-Benz factory in Marienfelde. There were also some exceptions, as happened in Kharkov after the recapture of the city in 1943 by the Das Reich Division. The SS captured a complex where the Russians had begun to produce T-34s, and the Germans used this to refit units inside the Division. However, the subject vehicle that appears in this chapter dates from 1944, which means that it was very likely converted in the field. During 1944 and 1945 the Germans were forced onto the defensive, making it more difficult for them to capture Russian tanks.

It is likely that only a few dozen T-34 747(r)-3s ever existed, perhaps fewer. I came across three sets of references for the (r)-3; some pictures of models modified by the Russians do exist, such as those used in Berlin or in the Czech Republic. The German denomination of captured tanks began with the number '700'; the letter in brackets following this referred to the country of origin ('r' for Russia in the case of the T-34); and the last number related to the version, which is '3' in the case of our winter tank. In spite of the great German interest in using captured tanks, only a few were ever used in battle. Thousands were used for replacement parts, and only a few hundred actually ended up in the service of the Reich.

The 747

You may find it surprising that a German T-34 has been included in this book ahead of some other more obvious choices. It is true that there were few of them, but in modelling terms the German T-34 punches above its weight. Numerous kits and aftermarket offerings in resin and plastic focus on Russian tanks in German service, and for this reason this 747(r)-3 has been included. It is also true that many of the modelling techniques and finishes shown in this chapter can be applied equally to both German and Allied armour.

A winter photo montage of the finished German 747(3)-r. (MJ)

This image features the original black and white reference picture used for inspiration. (MJ)

I also find Russian tanks captured and put into service by the Germans very inspiring for my modelling. Imagine the moment when a group of reconnaissance troops creep up on and capture that T-34, or a captured tank's journey to Germany or the Baltic countries for repair or refit, or when the modified T-34 faces up to its former Soviet owners in the field of battle for the first time – well, there's plenty of food for thought for some excellent dioramas and vignettes. One suggestion I might offer the reader is a diorama of a pulled-apart T-34 in a German factory, with the mechanics and engineers adapting the armour and accessories to transform it into an (r)-1 or an (r)-2. When the Germans did this, they numbered up all the pieces of the original tank, to make sure that all the pieces would fit together again correctly later. It could of course be possible that different T-34s from different factories could end up in the same repair plant, and that not all the components were interchangeable. In short, the possible scenarios are endless, giving more weight to the value of depicting captured tanks for the modeller, a sub-branch of modelling in its own right.

The base kit

At present, there is no outstanding kit of a T-34/76 with a hexagonal turret on the market. The old Tamiya kit may be the nearest thing to it, but it is a little out of date compared with the current high standards. I preferred to choose a more complicated alternative, but one that it is more correct and realistic. I used two Dragon kits of the T-34 as a base: the T-34/76 Model 1941 (6205) and the T-34/85 UTZ Model 1944 (6203). The upper hull came from the T-34/76; you cannot use the upper hull of the T-34/85 because the diameter of the turret ring is wider than that of the T-34/76, and some details of the engine covers are different. The dual-kit solution is not a cheap one, but makes the construction process a lot less complicated. Although both kits are from Dragon, the fit of the pieces is not perfect and both patience and putty will be required.

The turret used is a resin offering from TWS. Although it was intended for the Tamiya kit, it will suffice for our project. For the turret roof, the Tamiya kit of the T-34/76 Model 1943 offers two different examples. One is the 'Mickey Mouse' version with two identical hatches, and the other one contains the cupola. Almost all of the wheels are from the T-34/85, although I decided to add in some other examples to make the overall look a little more original.

I chose to use PART photoetch for my T-34. This Polish company offers excellent quality and is simpler to use than Aber products in my view. For the modeller who is not used to working with etched metal, I recommend PART products, although they can be hard to obtain. However, an Aber set was vital for making the back grille hatch on the engine fan. My friend and colleague Adam Wilder built the grille using a soldering iron to unite the different parts.

The conversion

This was the most interesting part of the project for me. I had to work out, from reference photos, how the turret armour and side supports should be arranged. Originally, this T-34 had side and turret armour. However, probably due to poor manufacture, our subject had lost its side armour some time previously. The original reference picture shows that the hidden side of the tank has possibly retained two pieces of armour at least, with one more on the turret and the surrounding rail. After a little thought, I decided to omit these three pieces, for lack of information on how they should be made. Modelling is always an interpretation of reality, and we can adapt reality to our own wishes and needs. Perhaps the most conservative modeller might disagree, but even when choosing the colours for painting a tank or weathering with mud, we should recall that a process of interpretation is under way. For me, enjoying modelling without thinking of 'what someone might say' is the most important thing.

In similar vein, I decided to add a NOTEK lamp that doesn't appear in the original reference picture, but which was very common on captured vehicles. When making such changes, being able to explain the reason for them is also vital. In this case, the reference pictures show a brand new headlight on the tank; my interpretation has the headlight damaged and without either glass or light bulb, reasoning that the crew perhaps added the NOTEK lamp at some later stage. The general state of the paint is also different in my model to that shown in the reference picture. Putting all these details together, and considering the absence of all the side armour, we reach the conclusion that the scale model follows the reality of the picture, but several days or weeks later on. This is one of the most fascinating aspects of scale-modelling: not only can a direct representation of a picture be made, but time can be moved forward or back accordingly too.

The armour surrounding the turret was made from a thin sheet of aluminium. Aluminium is easier to bend than brass or copper. The supports were made from plastic, and the lateral supports were made from spare sections from the PART photoetch set.

A view of the completed construction phase, prior to painting. (MJ)

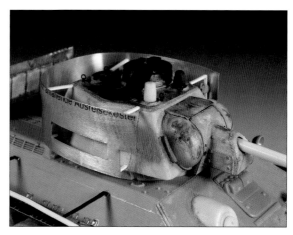

The left periscope is different to the right one, and is a later version. (MJ)

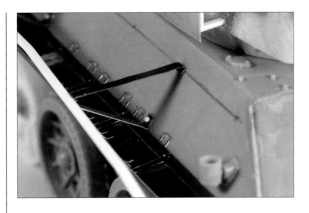

A detail of the side supports, made with spare metal from the PART photoetch set. (MJ)

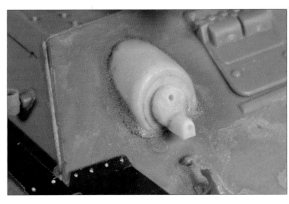

I used a resin replacement machine gun to improve the original kit offering. (MJ)

It is very easy to recreate damage on etched-metal fenders. All you need is a pair of pliers. (MJ)

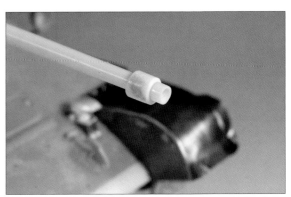

A detail of the cylinder added to the gun barrel, made with plasticard. (MJ)

I added two square fuel tanks from MIG Productions and a new cylindrical periscope in the roof of the turret. I also added a small scratchbuilt detail to the gun barrel. The Germans tried to simulate the Panzer IV Ausf. H with this conversion, and the overall aspect is very similar to the Ausf. H with the side and turret armour. Indeed, the profiles and silhouettes of the two are almost identical – and it is perhaps for this reason that there are no German identification crosses. To make the perfect 'clone', the Germans added a small cylinder to the end of the gun barrel to imitate the muzzle brake of the L48 German gun. The cylinder might simply be a can or an ammunition case, but it didn't improve the performance of the weapon in any way. However, it's a detail that makes this T-34 even more special.

Painting and weathering

Modellers are often fearful of tackling winter camouflage schemes, not knowing exactly how to begin. Should it be green first and white after, or vice versa? The best answer to such questions is 'take a look at the real thing'. If the green colour was applied first, and the Germans painted the tank white later, that's what modellers should do too. It is also the most logical and easiest order. But we should also remember that white is a more dominant colour. If the camouflage is heavily deteriorated and worn away, you should apply less white colour with your airbrush. The converse applies if the tank has been freshly painted. For this reason, it is important to set out the condition of your scale model from the start.

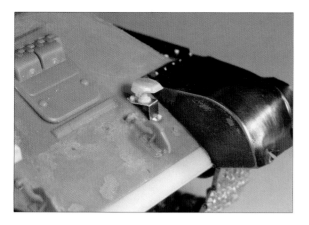

I added a NOTEK lamp from MIG Productions. The base is made from metal with some plastic rivets added. (MJ)

The headlight mounting bracket was made out of metal; the interior of the headlight was thinned out with a drill too. (MJ)

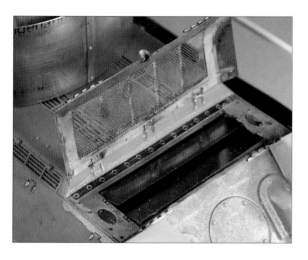

The interior cooling hatches are from the PART photoetch set, while the external metal grille is from Aber. (MJ)

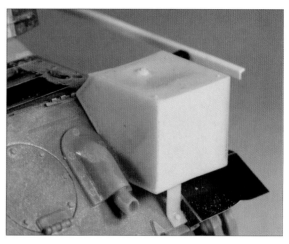

In order to attach the square fuel tank, the last rivet on the front hull had to be removed to allow for the mounting bracket to be fitted. (MJ)

The detail on the Tamiya cupola is poor, so this was improved by adding the visor parts from the Dragon T-34/85 UTZ kit. (MJ)

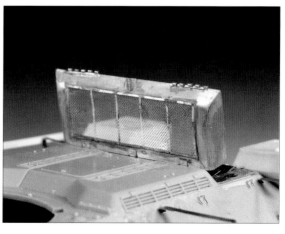

All the photoetch grille parts were soldered together, to ensure a firm bond (they can become unstuck if superglue is used). (MJ)

RIGHT Two of the left side wheels are early steel versions. I used resin ones but you can use the Tamiya kit ones too. (MJ)

BELOW AND OPPOSITE TOP Two views of the completed construction phase. (MJ)

Another area of concern regarding winter camouflage is when modellers think the tank should be very white. This is not always the case: for example, if you buy a new white T-shirt, how long does that brilliant whiteness actually last for? Imagine a pristine, white T-34 running at full speed through forests, down roads and across rivers; or with a dozen, muddy-booted Soviet troops hitching a ride into combat on top; or it being refuelled and repaired at the

greasy, oily depot; not to mention sitting out in freezing night rain and baking daytime sunshine. You get the picture – there will be little pure brilliant white left on a T-34 at the end of this lot. Part of the origin of this confusion lies in the fact that original pictures are in black and white, where the whiteness is exaggerated and everything else looks grey or black. We forget that what looks white might actually be another colour. This is especially the case when photographing an object in the snow, where the resulting picture is full of contrast and subtle shades are cancelled out. Modellers should always 'dirty' the white down and soften it, for the sake of realism. The images that follow show how to create a whitewash camouflage scheme in a simple and quick way, and how to weather the model.

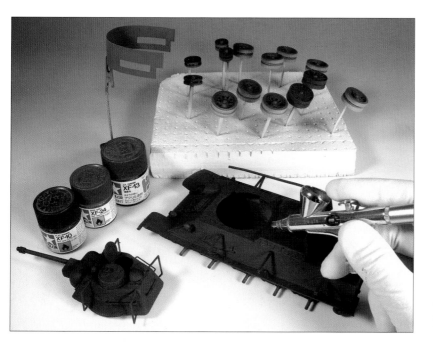

I start by painting the base colour using Tamiya Color paints. The turret armour has been painted dark grey on the outside, but flat brown inside. (MJ)

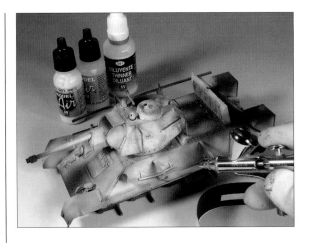

Next I apply some Vallejo white paint mixed with gloss varnish to certain areas in a random way, to create different depths. (MJ)

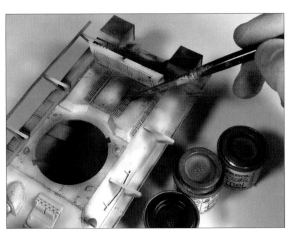

To create the first fading and chipping effect, I dry-brush on Humbrol enamels nos. 33, 86 and 98. (MJ)

The brush should move quickly and in a circular motion. (MJ)

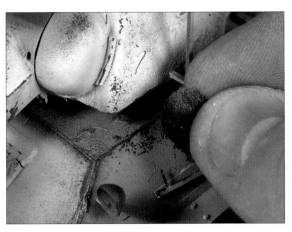

To create the first chips, here I am using the 'sponge' method. (MJ)

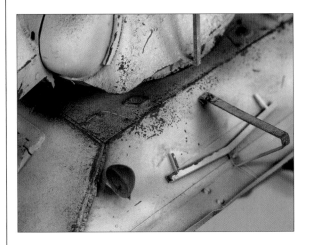

Go gently with this technique. Too much sponging can ruin your model. (MJ)

The sponge material should be firm; a good material to use is the packaging from electrical materials. Keep the sponge moist during painting, and wipe off any excess on absorbent paper before applying it to the model. (MJ)

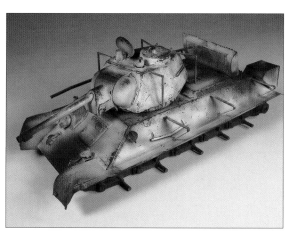

The results of the dry-brushing and sponge applications. (MJ)

Next we start to make a 'mapping' of white colour on the model, which consists of the overlap of different layers of stains. Dilute the paint when applying the white in this step. (MJ)

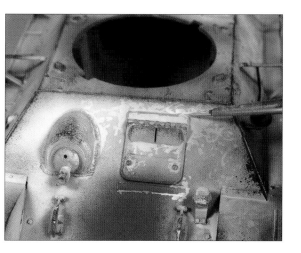

Don't worry about any excessive contrast at this stage. (MJ)

The final effect should be almost transparent. (MJ)

Some areas can be left untouched; you don't need to cover the whole surface with white. (MJ)

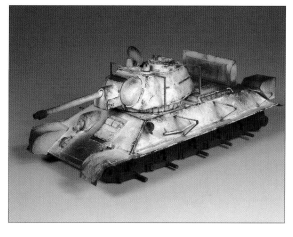

The 'white mapping' phase completed. (MJ)

Next we apply a filter. I have used the new SIN Industries filters which offer special colours for tanks, in this case Tan. (MJ)

You can apply the filter straight from the jar; remember to shake it first. It's a very transparent and stable medium. (MJ)

The hull with filter applied, and the turret without the filter. The difference is remarkable. The yellowish aspect will disappear after the steps to follow have been executed. (MJ)

Next we move to the washes. I use Abteilung modelling oils specifically for military vehicles blended with Humbrol. (MJ)

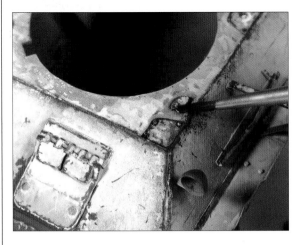

The Abteilung/Humbrol mix is thinned with odourless turpentine from Abteilung before application. (MJ)

A pin wash is applied to all the details, using a fine paintbrush. (MJ)

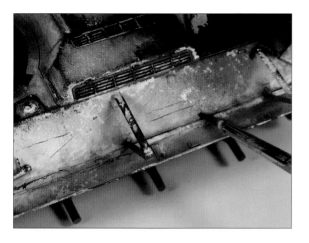

The wash will later be treated with a clean paintbrush and turpentine. (MJ)

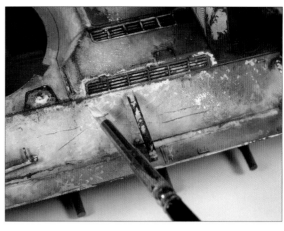

Next, more white colour, using Humbrol 34, is applied to the model. (MJ)

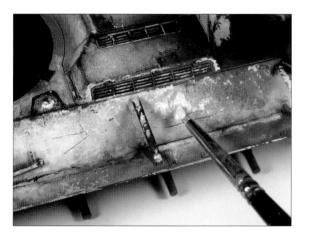

Some more irregular patches are created in the process. (MJ)

These new irregular patches are then blended in with turpentine. (MJ)

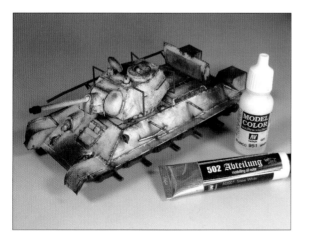

The chipping and 'patching' process has now been applied to all the surfaces of the model. (MJ)

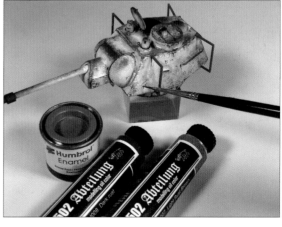

The rust colour for the model was made from a mix of Humbrol Enamel No. 62, and Dark Rust and Light Rust from Abteilung Modelling Oils. (MJ)

First we paint on some fine lines and scratches. (MJ)

Next the lines and scratches are smeared downwards and blended in with a clean paintbrush. (MJ)

To recreate wear on the horizontal areas, a dry-brushing of a mixture of dark brown (from oils and Humbrol) is applied. (MJ)

On the fenders, areas of brown wear and dirt are added. (MJ)

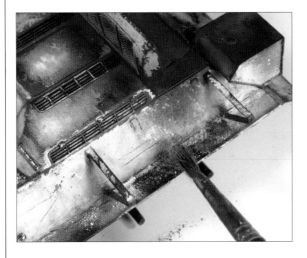

After allowing this to dry off, different coloured pigments are applied. (MJ)

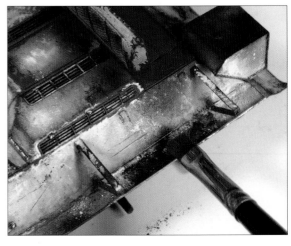

Then thinner for washes from MIG Productions is applied, to fix the pigment powders. (MJ)

To make the mud, pigments P028, P033, P034 and P027 are mixed with acrylic resin P032 and some garden soil. This is scooped up on an old paintbrush, and the mud is blown onto the tank with an airbrush. (MJ)

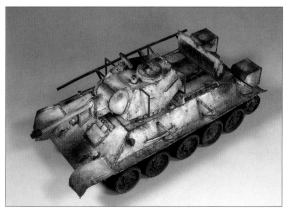

The model after the mud and dust have been applied. (MJ)

Be careful not to overdo the mud effect to the rear of the vehicle. (MJ)

Different mixtures of mud can be made to enrich the surface. Start with the lighter colours and finish with the darkest. (MJ)

The engine hatches were painted with rust colour pigments, blended and set with thinner. (MJ)

At least three or four colours need to be applied to achieve a realistic effect. (MJ)

The exhaust pipes are painted the same way as the engine hatches. (MJ)

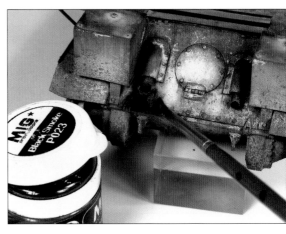

Black Smoke is then applied to represent the exhaust staining. (MJ)

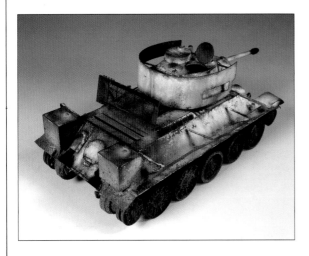

The rusting and exhaust staining phase finished. (MJ)

To recreate the effects of spilled oil, Humbrol 33 is mixed with Abteilung Oils Dark Rust, and a little gloss varnish. (MJ)

Using the 'spilled oil' mixture, some transparent initial stains diluted with turpentine are made. (MJ)

A second application of staining is made on top of these, but applied more carefully, darkening some areas of the original stains. (MJ)

The finished model. (MJ)

The finished model. (MJ)

The finished model. (MJ)

Bibliography and further reading

T-34 Medium Tank
1941–45

Steven Zaloga · Illustrated by Peter Sarson

Osprey Publishing's New Vanguard
9: T-34/76 Medium Tank 1941–45,
written by Steve Zaloga and
illustrated by Peter Sarson.

Bean, Tim and Fowler, Will *Russian Tanks of World War II: Stalin's Armored Might*, Motorbooks International, 2002.

Cornish, Nik *Images of Kursk: History's Greatest Tank Battle, July 1943*, Potomac Books, 2002.

Drabkin, Artem and Sheremet, Oleg *T-34 in Action*, Leo Cooper Ltd, 2006.

Ford, Roger and Hughes, Matthew *T-34 Russian Battle Tank*, Motorbooks International, 1999.

Hughes, Matthew and Mann, Chris *The T-34 Tank* (Weapons of War series), Spellmount Publishers Ltd, 1999.

Michulec, R., *T-34 Mityczna Bron*, Vols I and II, Armagedon Publishing.

Regenberg, Werner and Scheibert, Horst *Captured Tanks Under the German Flag: Russian Battle Tanks*, Schiffer Publishing, 1991.

Scheibert, Horst *The Russian T-34 Battle Tank*, Schiffer Publishing, 1992.

T34: Stalin's War-Horse, AJaKS Military Books (Poland), 2003.

T34 in Combat, AJaKS Military Books (Poland), 2003.

Zaloga, S. J. *Soviet Tanks and Combat Vehicles of World War Two*, Arms and Armour Press, 1984.

Zaloga, S. J. and Grandson, J., *T-34 Tank* (In Action series), Squadron/Signal Publications, Inc., 1983.

Zaloga, S. J. and Sarson, P., New Vanguard No. 9: *T-34/76 Medium Tank 1941–45*, Osprey Publishing, 1994.

Zaloga, S. J., Kinnear, J., Aksenov, A. and Koshchavtsev, A., *Soviet Tanks in Combat 1941–1945*, Concord Publications Co., 1997.

Kits and accessories

The T-34 is well served by kit manufacturers and aftermarket producers. To list all of the latter in particular would take up significant space, and would soon fall out of date. To this end, a list of complete kits at the time of going to press, across a variety of scales, is provided below for the T-34/76. Readers are advised to consult their hobby store or on-line hobby retailers for an up-to-date list of conversion and detailing parts from manufacturers such as Aber, PART, MIG Productions, Eduard, Moskit and Jordi Rubio.

Manufacturer	Kit no.	Scale	Description
Dragon	DN6205	1/35	T-34/76 Model 1941
Dragon	DN6185	1/35	T-34/76 German Army
Dragon	DN6092	1/35	T-34/76 Model 1940
Dragon	DN7266	1/72	T-34/76 Model 1942
Dragon	DN7258	1/72	T-34/76 Model 1940
Dragon	DN7259	1/72	T-34/76 Model 1941
Eastern Express	EA72053	1/72	T-34/76 with PT-3 mine roller
Eastern Express	EA72052	1/72	T-34/76 Model 1943 flamethrower
Eastern Express	EA72050	1/72	T-34/76 Model 1943 early
Eastern Express	EA72051	1/72	T-34/76 Model 1943 late
Fujimi	FU76021	1/76	Russian T-34/76
HAT Industrie	HAT99005	1/72	T-34/76 (two-pack)
Italeri	IT7008	1/72	T-34/76 Russian tank
Maquette	MQ3503	1/35	T-34 with 57mm Zis-4 AT gun
Maquette	MQ35036	1/35	T-34/D30, Arab-Israeli war
Maquette	MQ3504	1/35	T-34 Stalingrad production
Maquette	MQ3570	1/35	Flakpanzer T-34 747
Maquette	MQ3511	1/35	T-34/76 Model 1940
Maquette	MQ3512	1/35	T-34/76 Model 1941
Revell	RV3212	1/76	T-34/76 Model 1940
Tamiya	TA35059	1/35	T-34/76 Model 1943
Tamiya	TA35149	1/35	Russian T-34/76 'ChTZ' version, Model 1943
Trumpeter	TU00903	1/16	T-34/76 Model 1943
Trumpeter	TU00905	1/16	T-34/76 Model 1942
Unimodel	UNIM337	1/72	T-34/76 1940 with F-34 gun
Unimodel	UNIM325	1/72	T-34/76 Model 1942
Unimodel	UNIM329	1/72	T-34/76 Model 1941
Unimodel	UNIM336	1/72	T-34/76 Model 1940 with L-11 gun
Unimodel	UNIM331	1/72	OT-34 flamethrower version
Unimodel	UNIM326	1/72	T-34/76 Model 1943 with cast turret
Zvezda	ZVE3525	1/35	T-34/76
Zvezda	ZVE3535	1/35	T-34/76 Model 1942
Zvezda	ZVE3580	1/35	T-34/76 with mine roller

Index

Figures in **bold** refer to illustrations